I Pledge Allegiance To the King

A New Testament Theology of the Christian Life

Dennis Ingolfsland

An imprint of
GLOBALEDADVANCEPRESS

I PLEDGE ALLEGIANCE TO THE KING
A New Testament Theology of the Christian Life

Library of Congress Control Number: 2013955471

Ingolfsland, Dennis 1954 -
I PLEDGE ALLEGIANCE TO THE KING
A New Testament Theology of the Christian Life

ISBN 978-1-935434-21-4

Subject Codes and Description:
   Subject Codes and Description: 1. REL 006070 Religion – Biblical Commentary -- New Testament; 2. REL 006220 – RELIGION—Biblical Studies – New Testament;; 3. REL 067040 Religion: Christian Theology - Christology

ESV and NIV translations of the Bible were used in this book.
Cover design by Brian Lane Green
Printed in Australia, Brazil, France, Germany, Italy, Spain, UK, and USA.

Published by
Post-Gutenberg Books[tm]
an imprint of
GlobalEdAdvance Press

www.GlobalEdAdvance.org

Dedicated to my family:

To Sheila, my devoted wife of 39 years

To my wonderful children and children-in-law:
Jason, Melinda, Kevin and Sarah

To my adorable grand-children:
Lucy, Wyatt, Sawyer, Autumn, Parker,
Eli and Alijah
And in memory of Aiden

TABLE OF CONTENTS

PART I: INTRODUCING THE KING

PART II: SERVING THE KING

PART I

Introducing The King

Introduction

In *The Patriot*, a movie about the Revolutionary War, Mel Gibson's character stands up in a town meeting to oppose the looming war with Britain. He asks why he should trade one tyrant 3,000 miles away for 3,000 tyrants one mile away. The line is a good illustration of the fact that while Americans tend to view monarchy unfavorably, many in history would not have held the same views. Our views of monarchy are colored not only by history lessons of the tyrannical King George, from whom we seceded, but by stories of modern tyrants who trample peoples' rights. It is an undeniable fact, however, that democracies can also trample on people's rights just as surely as dictatorships or monarchies.

In the ancient Jewish world people didn't think in terms of democracies. At one time they demanded a king like all the other nations.[1] Some kings they loved. Some kings they hated. [2] When they had a king they hated, they dreamed not of replacing him with a democracy, but of the day when God would replace him with an all-wise, just, and compassionate King—the Messiah or Christ. The word "Messiah" comes from a Hebrew word meaning to anoint. As Kostenberger notes, "Anointed' designates the special ceremony of installing an individual to an exalted position, most notably that of king or ruler."[3]

---

1   1 Samuel 8:5-20.
2   King Ahaziah and King Amaziah, for example, were assassinated.
3   Kostenberger, Andreas. *A Theology of John's Gospel and Letters.* (Grand Rapids: Zondervan, 2009). 313. Kostenberger cites the following passages in support: First Samuel 9:15-16; 10:1; 16:3, 12-13; Second Samuel 2:4; 5:3; First Kings 1:34, 45; 5:1; Second Kings 9:3, 6; 11:12; 23-30. Kostenberger goes on to point out that "Anointed" is also sometimes used of the patriarchs (Psalm 105:15) and prophets or priests (Exodus 28:41; Leviticus 4:3-5; Numbers 3:3; first Kings 19:16).

According to the New Testament, Jesus was this long-awaited Jewish Messiah or "King of Kings." The New Testament also presents Jesus as the fulfillment of Old Testament prophecies about God visiting his people. In this book, part one will argue that not only does the New Testament teach such things about Jesus, but contrary to many modern critics Jesus actually taught these things about himself.

If anyone, however, actually made such exalted claims about himself, wouldn't people be more likely to believe that he was crazy than to become his followers? In fact, why would *anyone* believe that a Galilean peasant was a divine King? Do we have any reasons to believe that New Testament teaching about Jesus is true, or is it just a matter of blind faith? Part one will explore these questions.

Assuming that Jesus really was the long-awaited King of Kings, part two will explore the question of what Jesus demanded from his subjects. Some scholars believe that Jesus' message was fundamentally different from the gospel Paul preached.[4] For example, the Gospels seem to emphasize obedience even for salvation, while Paul seems to emphasize grace. Were Jesus and Paul in contradiction? What exactly did Jesus and Paul believe about salvation?

Churches often talk about "accepting Christ," or making a decision for Christ," or "trusting Christ," or "asking Jesus into your heart;" but to many people these phrases are little more than clichés. What do they really mean? And what relationship is there, if any, between faith/trust/belief in Christ and obedience or good works? Even Evangelicals have strongly disagreed on these issues.[5] Finally, are these issues just

---

4   See, for example, Tabor, James D. Paul and Jesus; How the Apostle Transformed Christianity. (New York : Simon and Schuster, 2012).

5   For two opposite perspectives see for example, John MacArthur. *The Gospel according to Jesus: What is Authentic Faith*. Rev. ed. (Grand Rapids: Zondervan, 2008) and Zane Hodges. *Absolutely Free; A Biblical Reply to Lordship Salvation*. (Grand Rapids : Zondervan, 1989).

esoteric academic discussions or do they have any practical relevance to the Christian life? Part two will answer these questions. As we shall see, the answers are not only intensely practical but have eternal significance as well.

Because this book is so extensively documented with Scripture, Scripture passages have been placed in footnotes rather than in the text. To have hundreds of Scripture citations in the text would be distracting to the reader. Since this book is intended primarily for college freshmen and church laypeople, other footnotes contain explanatory discussions that may not be clear to those who are not pastors or New Testament professors. Footnotes also contain occasional comments on the Greek text for pastors and others who have taken Greek.

Chapter One

The Expectation of the King

Although Jewish people before Jesus' time seemed to have different views about what their coming Messiah would be like[6] a prominent view in Jesus' day was that the Messiah was going to be a king, a descendant of King David. In fact, the Messiah was to be the ultimate king—the king of all kings,[7] the one whom even King David, the greatest of Israel's kings, would call, "lord."[8]

The roots of this idea can be found in the Old Testament. For example, Isaiah predicted the coming of one who would "be called Wonderful Counselor, Mighty God, Everlasting Father, Prince of Peace" and who would "reign on David's throne and over his kingdom, establishing it and upholding it with justice and righteousness" forever.[9]

Jeremiah predicted that God would raise up "a righteous branch" or descendant of King David. According to Jeremiah this righteous descendant would be "A King who will reign wisely and do what is just and right in the land." Jeremiah said his name would be called "Yahweh our Righteousness."[10] Micah predicted the coming of a ruler out of Bethlehem whose "greatness will reach the ends of the earth" and who will cause Israel to dwell securely.[11]

---

6   For example in the Dead Sea Scrolls there is mention of two messiahs, a Messiah of David (or kingly Messiah) and a Messiah of Aaron (or priestly Messiah). See Vanderkam, James C. *The Dead Sea Scrolls Today*. (Grand Rapids : Eerdmans, 1994), 117-118. In the New Testament we find both of these ideas combined in Jesus.
7   Revelation 17:14; 19:16; cf. First Timothy 6:15.
8   Matthew 22:44; Mark 12:36; Luke 20:42; Acts 2:34 all quoting from Psalm 110:1.
9   Isaiah 9:6-7.
10   Jeremiah 23:5-6.
11   Micah 5:2-5.

This idea of a future Messiah-king is also found in other Jewish literature of Jesus' time. For example, the first century BC book of *1 Enoch*, speaks of a Messiah called the "Son of Man," the "Chosen One," who will be "a staff for the righteous ones...to lean on."[12] He will be one whom "All those who dwell on the earth shall fall and worship before him,"[13] but those who deny the Lord and "his Messiah" "shall burn before the face of the holy ones."[14]

Similarly, this idea of a kingly Messiah is also found in the first century AD *Psalms of Solomon* (not the biblical book of Psalms) which says, "See, Lord, and raise up for them their king, the son of David, to rule over your servant Israel."[15] The *Psalms of Solomon* adds that he "will be a righteous king over them, taught by God. There will be no unrighteousness among them in his days for all shall be holy, and their king shall be the Lord Messiah."[16]

---

12   1 Enoch 48:4.
13   1 Enoch 48:2-7.
14   1 Enoch 48:8-10.
15   Psalms of Solomon 17:21.
16   Psalms of Solomon 17:32.

Chapter Two

The King
in the Gospels

This Jewish expectation of a Messiah is also found in the Gospels. For example, in the Gospel of Luke, when Mary was told by the angel that she would give birth to a son, the angel said, "The Lord God will give him the throne of his father David, and he will reign over the house of Jacob forever; his kingdom will never end."[17] According to Matthew, the wise men came to Herod and asked, "Where is he who has been born king of the Jews?"[18] In the Gospel of John, Nathaniel said to Jesus, "Rabbi, you are the Son of God! You are the King of Israel!"[19] Later in Jesus' ministry, after he had fed five thousand men, he perceived that the people were about to "take him by force to make him king."[20]

The idea, therefore, that the Messiah or Christ would be the ultimate and final King was apparently common in Jesus day, and it seems pretty clear from the Gospels that this is precisely who Jesus claimed to be—though he seems to have been very careful about how he made this known. He never went around saying, "Excuse me. Can I have your attention? I am the Christ!" For someone to publicly proclaim himself to be the Christ, making a big deal of it, may have greatly concerned the Romans who may have ended his ministry before his time had come. But although Jesus was careful about how he

---

17   Luke 1:32-33
18   Matthew 2:2.
19   John 1:49.
20   John 6:15.

revealed that he was the Messiah, he did not hide it and was quite clear. For example, Jesus did not deny it when Peter said to Jesus, "You are the Christ."[21] In fact, according to Matthew's Gospel, Jesus said Peter was blessed because it was God who had revealed that to Peter.[22]

Near the end of Jesus' ministry (in one of the few stories found in all four Gospels) Jesus rode into Jerusalem on a donkey.[23] Matthew says this was in fulfillment of a prophecy given some 400 years earlier by Zechariah who wrote:

> Rejoice greatly, O daughter of Zion! Shout aloud, O daughter of Jerusalem! Behold *your king is coming to you*; righteous and having salvation is he, humble and mounted on a donkey, on a colt, the foal of a donkey.[24]

According to both Luke and John, the people witnessing this event hailed Jesus as the king.[25] What is interesting about the Zechariah prophecy is that it is about Israel's king coming to them on a donkey, but in Zechariah, the king is God himself![26] Jesus was not only presenting himself as Israel's king, but he was claiming to fulfill prophecies about God coming to his people.[27] The idea that Jesus consciously

---

21   Mark 8:29; cf. Matthew 16:15-20 and Luke 9:20-21.
22   Matthew 16:17.
23   Matthew 21:1-9; Mark 11:1-10; Luke 19:28-40; John 12:12-19.
24   Zechariah 9:9. Emphasis mine.
25   John 12:13; Luke 19:38.
26   Zechariah 14:9, 16. The idea that God is the ultimate King is found numerous times in the Old Testament. For example, "Give attention to the sound of my cry, my King and my God, for to you do I pray" (Psalm 5:2). "The Lord is king forever and ever" (Psalm 10:16). "Who is this King of glory? The Lord, strong and mighty" (Psalm 24:8). "The Lord sits enthroned as king forever" (Psalm 29:10). "You are my King, O God" (Psalm 44:4). "For the Lord, the Most High, is to be feared, a great king over all the earth" (Psalm 47:2). "For God is the King of all the earth; sing praises with a psalm!" (Psalm 47:7); et al. "The LORD is our king, he will save us" (Isaiah 33:22). "I am the Lord, your Holy One, the Creator of Israel, your King" (Isaiah 43:15). "Thus says the Lord, the King of Israel" (Isaiah 44:6). "But the Lord is the true God; he is the living God and the everlasting King" (Jeremiah 10:10). "As I live, declares the Lord God, surely with a mighty hand and an outstretched arm and with wrath poured out I will be king over you" (Ezekiel 20:33). "The King of Israel, the Lord, is in your midst" (Zephaniah 3:15). "For I am a great King, says the Lord of hosts" (Malachi 1:14).
27   See Wright, N.T. Jesus and the Victory of God (Minneapolis : Fortress Press, 1996), 653.

thought of himself as fulfilling prophecies about God coming to his people is supported in numerous passages; more on this in the next chapter.

For Jesus to present himself as King, and for the people to proclaim him as such, would certainly have been seen as highly subversive by the Romans. In fact, Jesus' claim to be king actually became an issue in his trials. He was first tried before the Sanhedrin or "chief priests"[28] where the high priest asked him, "Are you the Christ, the Son of the Blessed?"[29] Jesus' answer was very clear, "I am; and you will see the Son of Man seated at the right hand of Power, and coming with the clouds of heaven."[30]

Jesus' reference to coming in the clouds of heaven was a clear allusion to a prophecy given in the book of Daniel, written long before Jesus' time, which spoke of a "son of man" who would be given an eternal kingdom over all the earth:

> I saw in the night visions, and behold, with the clouds of heaven there came one like a son of man, and he came to the Ancient of Days and was presented before him. And to him was given *dominion and glory and a kingdom* that all peoples, nations, and languages should serve him; his dominion is *an everlasting dominion* which shall not pass away and *his kingdom* one that shall not be destroyed.[31]

Jesus was claiming to be that King. After pronouncing Jesus guilty of blasphemy and worthy of death,[32] the Jewish leaders sent him to the Roman governor, Pontius Pilate.[33] The Roman governor, of course would care nothing about Jewish blasphemy charges but he would be very concerned about

---

28   Matthew 26:57-68; Mark 14:53-65; Luke 22:54-71; John 18:13-24.
29   i.e. God; Mark 14:61; Matthew 26:63; Luke 22:67.
30   Mark 14:62; cf. Matthew 26:64; Luke 22:67-69.
31   Daniel 7:13-14. Emphasis mine.
32   Matthew 26:65-66; Mark 14:64.
33   The Jews could not legally put anyone to death without Roman approval. The only exception was if a Gentile entered the inner courts of the Temple.

someone claiming to be king. In all four Gospels, Pilate's question to Jesus was, therefore, "Are you the King of the Jews?"[34]

In the Synoptic Gospels (Matthew, Mark and Luke), Jesus' answer, "You have said so," seems a little ambiguous."[35] Some have interpreted this as "your words, not mine" but it seems more likely that this was an idiom similar to our expression, "You said it!" which, of course, means yes! That "yes" is precisely what Jesus meant is clarified by John who adds that Jesus affirmed his kingship telling Pilate, "My kingship is not of this world; if my kingship were of this world, my servants would fight...."[36] In other words, Jesus did not deny he was a king, he just said that his kingdom was not [yet] of this world. That Jesus believed his kingdom would one day be "of this world" seems clear from some of his parables and other teaching.[37] In any case, Pilate concluded that this peasant was no threat to Rome and told Jesus' accusers, "I find no crime in him."[38]

Pilate then offered to release either Jesus or the insurrectionist, Barabbas.[39] Pilate asked, "Do you want me to release for you the King of the Jews?"[40] When the people called for the release of Barabbas, Pilate asked, "then what shall I do with the man whom you call King of the Jews?"[41] The crowd called out, "Crucify Him!"[42]

---

34   Matthew 27:11; Mark 15:2; Luke 23:3; John 18:33.
35   Matthew 27:11; Mark 15:2; Luke 23:3.
36   John 18:36.
37   For example, Matthew 25:41-46; Luke 19:11-27
38   Luke 23:4; John 18:38.
39   Matthew 27:15-23; Mark 15:6-14; Luke 23:17-23; John 18:39-40. Although some critics have questioned the historicity of this event, all four Gospels record it and Craig Evans has pointed out that other governors had done similar things in Jesus' time (Craig Evans and N.T. Wright. *Jesus the final days*. [Louisville, KY : WJK Press, 2009]. 21.
40   Mark 15:9; John 18:39.
41   Mark 15:12.
42   Some critics have questioned the historicity of this pointing out that just days earlier the crowds had hailed Jesus as king so it seems unlikely—to them—that they would so

The Gospel of John adds an additional element to the story. According to John, Pilate had sought to release Jesus but the crowd said, "If you release this man, you are not Caesar's friend; everyone who makes himself a king sets himself against Caesar."[43] Pilate asked, "Shall I crucify your king?" and the crowd responded, "We have no king but Caesar."[44]

So Barabbas was released and Jesus was handed over to the soldiers to be crucified. The soldiers clearly understood that Jesus was being executed for his claim to be a king. They showed their contempt for Jesus by spitting on him, by putting a purple royal robe on him and a crown woven with thorns on his head, and by mocking him saying "Hail King of the Jews."[45]

When Jesus was crucified, Pilate had ordered that an inscription be placed on the cross to read, "King of the Jews."[46] While on the cross, Jesus was mocked by people who asked why he didn't just come down off the cross if he were really the "King of Israel" or Christ.[47] The soldiers joined in saying, "If you are King of the Jews, save yourself!"[48]

If that were the end of the matter this would be the story of a poor peasant who thought he was a king and died because of his delusions of grandeur. Jesus' claims, however, were vindicated in the minds of his followers when on the third day they saw him alive and well, risen from the dead

---

soon call for his crucifixion. The critics are not thinking from a first century context. Jesus had just come into Jerusalem in fulfillment of Zechariah's prophecy about Israel's King coming to them riding on a donkey. The people were hoping that this famous wonder-working prophet from Galilee really was their Messiah and that he would soon move—maybe at this Passover feast—to deliver them from the Romans. When they saw this same man, just days later, beaten and bloodied and chained between two Roman soldiers they concluded that he was an impostor—it just wasn't possible, they reasoned, that their King, the Messiah, could be defeated by the Romans. So they turned on him with a vengeance. Contrary to some critics, the story makes perfect historical sense.

43 John 19:12.
44 John 19:15.
45 Matthew 27:28-31; Mark 15:17-20; John 19:2-3.
46 Matthew 27:37; Mark 15:26; Luke 23:38; John 19:19.
47 Matthew 27:42; Mark 15:31-32; Luke 23:35.
48 Luke 23:37.

(More on this later). According to the Gospels, Jesus' disciples not only saw him after his death, but had conversations with him, touched him and even ate with him.

Still not sure what to make of all this, his disciples asked, him, "Lord, will you at this time restore the kingdom to Israel?" They understood from the Tanakh (the Christian Old Testament) that the Messiah, the King, would set up his kingdom on earth. Jesus' answer implied that they were right about the Messiah setting up his kingdom. In other words, Jesus did not deny that he would restore the kingdom to Israel; he just said that it was not for them to know the timing. In the meantime, they were to go into all the world and make disciples, baptizing them and teaching them to obey Jesus' commands.[49]

This understanding of Jesus as the King—which, along with the resurrection, is the climax of the entire Gospel story—helps to put other Gospel passages in perspective. For example, virtually all Jesus scholars agree that one of the most prominent themes in the Gospels is the kingdom of God. For example, the very first words that both Matthew and Mark record of Jesus' preaching are "Repent, for the kingdom of God is at hand."[50] According to Luke 4:33, Jesus said he was sent for the purpose of preaching the good news of the kingdom of God.

Jesus taught that people should "seek first the Kingdom of God and his righteousness...."[51] When a rich young ruler asked Jesus what he had to do to have eternal life, Jesus told him to sell his possessions, give the money to the poor, and follow him. When the man declined, Jesus told his disciples, "How hard it will be for those who have riches to enter the

---

49   Acts 1:6-8; Matthew 28:18-20.
50   Mark 1:15. Matthew says the same thing, only substituting "Kingdom of Heaven" for Kingdom of God—Jews in Jesus' day would sometimes avoid saying or writing "God."
51   Mt 6:33.

kingdom of God."[52] All three Gospels that tell this story equate the kingdom of God with eternal life.[53]

A significant percentage of the Synoptic Gospels consist of Jesus' parables about the Kingdom of God.[54] In one such parable, Jesus spoke about a time when the Son of Man (a phrase Jesus often used to refer to himself) would come "in his glory and all the angels with him." Jesus said that at this time, he "will separate people one from another as a shepherd separates the sheep from the goats." Then "the King," who in the parable is Jesus,[55] will invite the sheep to:

> "inherit the kingdom prepared for you from the foundation of the world, For I was hungry and you gave me food, I was thirsty and you gave me drink, I was a stranger and you welcomed me, I was naked and you clothed me, I was sick and you visited me, I was in prison and you came to me."[56]

That the "sheep" did not do these good deeds in order to enter the kingdom (i.e. to become saved) is clear by the fact that they didn't even realize what they had done. They replied, "When did we see you a stranger and welcome you, or naked and clothe you," etc. Jesus, referring to himself, said, "The King will answer them, Truly I say to you, as you did it to the least of these my brothers, you did it to me."[57] In other words, their good deeds were the fruit or result of their relationship with the King, not the cause of their relationship. The King then sent the "goats" into "the eternal fire prepared for the devil and his angels."[58]

According to Luke, Jesus told another parable to

---

52   Mark 10:17-31//Matthew 19:16-30//Luke 18:18-30.
53   Matthew 19:29//Mark 10:30//Luke 18:30.
54   For example, Matthew 13:10-17 // Mark 4:10-12//Luke 8:9-10; Mark 4:26-29; Matthew 12:24-30; Matthew 13:31-32//Mark 4:30-32//Luke 13:18-19); Matthew 12:33//Luke 13:20-21; Matthew 22:7-14; Matthew 18:21-35; Matthew 25:1-13.
55   Matthew 25:34.
56   Matthew 25:34-36.
57   Matthew 25:37-39, 44.
58   Matthew 25:41-46.

address the fact that people expected the kingdom of God to come soon.[59] Jesus spoke of a nobleman who "went into a far country to receive for himself a kingdom and then return." This would probably have reminded them of Archelaus, the son of Herod the Great[60] who, after his father's death, went off to Rome expecting to be proclaimed king. In Jesus' parable the nobleman called ten of his servants and gave them ten minas (about two-years' wages for a laborer) and told them to "engage in business until I come." In the parable, as in the real life of Archelaus, "his citizens hated him and sent a delegation after him saying, 'We do not want this man to reign over us."

When the nobleman in the parable returned, he rewarded his servants for their faithful stewardship, except for one lazy servant who wouldn't even invest the money entrusted to him by his lord. The nobleman ordered that one to be slaughtered along with "these enemies of mine, who did not want me to reign over them...."[61] This parable about the Kingdom of God indicates that Jesus, like the nobleman, expected to go away for a time and then return to judge his subjects. In the meantime he expects his servants to be faithful.

One of the main themes of all four Gospels, therefore, is about Jesus the Christ or King, coming to his people with his good news of the kingdom. This story is brought to a climax in all four gospels with Jesus being executed for claiming to be the King of that kingdom, and being vindicated by his resurrection from the dead! We might be tempted to dismiss the entire story as the delusions of a Galilean peasant were it not for the fact that his resurrection is so well supported

---

59   Luke 19:11-27.
60   Herod the Great is the Herod in the Gospels who tried to have the baby Jesus killed.
61   Luke 19:11-27.

historically (more on this later).[62]

This message of Jesus' kingship or Messiahship continued even after his death. When Paul, for example, was preaching in Thessalonica, one of the charges made against Paul and his group was that they were "all acting against the decrees of Caesar saying that there is another king, Jesus."[63] Paul himself called Jesus "Christ," (i.e. Messiah) hundreds of times. Jesus is also called Christ in James, 1 Peter, 2 Peter, 1 John, 2 John, Jude and Revelation. Remember, Christ is not the last name of Jesus. The Christ was to be the final, ultimate King of all kings which is why both Paul and the book of Revelation call Jesus the "King of Kings and Lord of Lords."[64]

---

62   See, for example, **Scholarly discussion**: N.T. Wright. *The Resurrection of the Son of God*. (Minneapolis : Fortress Press, 2003); Michael R. Licona. *The Resurrection of Jesus; A New Historiographical Approach.* (Downers Grove, IL : IVP Press, 2010); **Easier reading:** Gary R. Habermas. *The Case for the Resurrection of Jesus.* (Grand Rapids : Kregel, 2004); Lee Strobel. *The Case for the Resurrection.* (Grand Rapids : Zondervan, 2010). **Debates**: William Lane Craig and Gerd Ludemann. *Jesus' Resurrection; Fact of Figment?* Edited by Paul Copan and Ronald K. Tacelli. (Downers Grove, IL: IVP Press, 2000); John Dominic Crossan and N.T. Wright. *The Resurrection of Jesus; John Dominic Crossan and N.T. Wright in Dialogue.* Edited by Robert B. Stewart (Minneapolis : Fortress Press, 2006). Gary Habermas and Antony Flew. *Did Jesus Rise from the Dead; The Resurrection Debate.* (Wipf and Stock, 2003).

63   Acts 17:7.

64   1 Tim 6:15, Revelation 17:14; 19:16.

Chapter Three

The Deity of the King
In the Gospels

According to the New Testament, Jesus was not only King of kings and Lord of lords, he was the very incarnation (or embodiment) of God. The writer of Mark—which most scholars believe to the first canonical gospel[65] to be written—began his gospel with quotes from Malachi 3:1 and Isaiah 40:3 about how a messenger would go before and prepare the way for Yahweh (God). After these quotes, Mark introduced John the Baptist who was preparing the way for Jesus.[66] Mark intended his readers to understand that Jesus is the fulfillment of the prophecy about the coming of God being announced by a messenger who Mark identified as John the Baptist.

Now in case that point was lost on some readers, Mark then wrote about how Jesus was baptized as the Spirit of God descended on him like a dove, and a voice came from the heavens declaring that Jesus is "my beloved Son." This declaration from God that Jesus is God's Son is repeated later in Mark 9:7.

It is important to note that "Son of God" (as Jesus is called in most ancient texts of Mark 1:1) can mean different things depending on the context. In Job, "sons of God" is a reference to angels.[67] Sometimes in the Old Testament, Israel was said to be God's son.[68] Sometimes the king was said to be

---

65   Canonical gospels are the four Gospels in the New Testament, as opposed to about thirty other non-canonical gospels written well over a hundred years after Jesus' time.
66   Mark 1:4-9.
67   Job 1:6
68   E.g. Exodus 4:22-23; Deuteronomy 1:31, 32:6; Jeremiah 3:19, 20; Hosea 11:1.

God's son. Mark, however, made it clear that Jesus is the son of God in a much more significant sense. In Mark 2:1-12 Jesus healed a paralyzed man and told him, "My son, your sins are forgiven."[69] Note that Jesus was not saying that this man has personally offended Jesus therefore Jesus forgives him of this offense. Jesus was not even acting as a priest by assuring the man of God's forgiveness. Mark wanted readers to understand that Jesus was declaring that this man's sins were forgiven. In a Jewish context only God could forgive sins; and remember, Jesus was a Jew who lived with and ministered to Jews.

According to Mark, the people understood exactly what Jesus was claiming because they complained saying, "He is blaspheming! Who can forgive sins but God alone."[70] Jesus then confirmed that this is exactly what he was teaching. Jesus told them that he said this so they would know that he had authority "on earth" to forgive sins. Jesus then commanded the paralyzed man to get up and walk...and the man did![71] Mark clearly intended his readers to understand that Jesus was claiming to do something only God could do—and Mark records that Jesus backed his claim up with a miracle.

To emphasize this point further, Mark then told a story about how Jesus had a run-in with Pharisees about picking grain on the Sabbath day in which Jesus claimed that he is Lord over the Sabbath.[72] This would have been a truly shocking claim, something that would have made Jesus sound like he was out of his mind. God instituted the Sabbath day and only God was above the Sabbath! Yet according to Mark, Jesus claimed to be Lord over the Sabbath. Mark clearly wanted readers to understand that Jesus was placing himself in the position of God.

---

69   Mark 2:5
70   Mark 2:7.
71   Mark 2:9-12.
72   Mark 2:23-28.

Mark later wrote about how Jesus taught people about Jewish dietary laws. Jesus said, "Do you not see that whatever goes into a person from outside cannot defile him, since it enters not his heart but his stomach and is expelled?" Mark then added his own parenthetical, theological explanation, "Thus he declared all foods clean."[73] This is another shocking statement. God had established those dietary laws! Only God could annul such laws. Again, Mark wanted the reader to understand that Jesus was claiming to do what only God could do.

In the Old Testament, God alone was the source of salvation in a spiritual sense, but in the Gospels, Jesus claimed that prerogative. According to Mark 10:17-21 a man asked Jesus how to have eternal life and Jesus' answer was "follow me." This is remarkable. None of the prophets—not Moses, not Elijah, not Isaiah—none of the prophets would have said that the way to have eternal life was to follow them. The prophets all pointed people to God. Only Jesus said the way to eternal life is to follow him!

But Mark was not done yet. He recorded that just before Jesus' death Jesus had a last supper with his disciples. Jesus took the cup of wine and told his disciples, "This is my blood of the covenant which is poured out for many."[74] The covenant to which Jesus was referring is from Jeremiah 31:31 which specifically declared that it will be Yahweh (God) who makes this covenant. Mark wanted the reader to understand that Jesus was, once again, putting himself in the place of God. It is no wonder some thought he was out of his mind![75]

Finally, as mentioned above, some four hundred years before Jesus' time, Zechariah prophesied to Israel, "Behold

---

73   Mark 7:18-19.
74   Mark 14:22-25.
75   Mark 3:21.

your king is coming to you; righteous and having salvation is he, humble and mounted on a donkey, on a colt, the foal of a donkey".[76] Zechariah told readers exactly who the king was: "And Yahweh will be king over all the earth".[77] Mark presented Jesus as deliberately fulfilling that prophecy about Israel's king coming to them by riding in to Jerusalem on a donkey.[78]

These views were not just expressed in the Gospel of Mark, however. Luke 7:47-50 and John 8:24 also claim that Jesus could personally grant forgiveness of sins. Matthew 12:8 and Luke 6:5 claim that Jesus was Lord over the Sabbath. Matthew 25:21-46 and Luke 19:11-27 claim that people's eternal destiny would be dependent on Jesus.[79] According to Matthew[80] and Luke[81] Jesus claimed that he would personally judge the world. All of these are the prerogatives of God alone. And all four Gospels[82] tell of Jesus riding into Jerusalem in fulfillment of the prophecies about God visiting his people. It is clear that what the synoptic Gospel writers want readers to understand is that Jesus is the God-King who has come to his people.

But all that is in the Synoptic gospels.[83] What about the Gospel of John? There is really not much dispute among biblical scholars that the Gospel of John intends to present Jesus as God incarnate (in the flesh). The only ones who dispute this are those with a theological axe to grind, for example, cults[84] like Jehovah's witnesses, etc.

---

76   Zechariah 9:9.
77   Zechariah 14:9, cf. 14:17.
78   Mark 11:1-10.
79   cf. John 3:15, 10:19; Gospel of Thomas 82.
80   Matthew 13:24-30; 36-43; 25:31-46.
81   Luke 3:16-17; 17:23-37.
82   Matthew 21:1-11; Mark 11:1-10; Luke 19:28-44; and John 12:12-19.
83   The "Synoptic Gospels" are Matthew, Mark and Luke. The word "synoptic" comes from two Greek words meaning "to see together. Matthew, Mark and Luke are called the Synoptic Gospels because they are so similar, even word-for-word identical in some places.
84   Technically a cult is just a religious sect or a system of worship rituals. In popular language, a Christian cult is a religious system that significantly deviates from foundational Christian doctrines, like the deity of Christ or the Trinity. Orthodox Christians have always

John begins his gospel declaring, "In the beginning was the Word, and the Word was with God and the Word was God. He was in the beginning with God. All things were made through him, and without him was not anything made that was made".[85] Then John declares that this "Word" which... was God, became human and lived with us.[86] He is the one to whom John the Baptist bore witness,[87] the one who is specifically identified as Jesus in John 1:29. Jesus is called, "the only God who is at the Father's side" in John 1:18.[88]

The fact that John attributes deity to Jesus is not just seen in chapter one, however. According to John's gospel, people's eternal destiny would be dependent on Jesus.[89] In a first century Jewish context only God could save in a spiritual sense. Only God could grant eternal life. According to John 8:58 Jesus claimed, "Truly, truly I say to you, before Abraham was, I AM." Not only did Jesus claim to have existed before his birth—a claim he also made in John 17:5—many scholars note that the phrase "I AM" is the name of God, Yahweh. This claim may be why, according to the text, Jesus enemies "picked up stones to throw at him."[90]

considered Jehovah's Witnesses and Mormons, for example, to be cults. On the other side, Jehovah's Witnesses and Mormons have generally considered themselves to be the true and faithful church, and have thought of orthodox Christians as having departed from the true faith.

85   John 1:1-3.
86   John 1:14.
87   John 1:15.
88   Jehovah's witnesses try to avoid this teaching by mistranslating John 1:1. Their *New World Translation* of John 1:1 reads, "In [the] beginning the Word was, and the Word was with God, and the Word was a god." Jehovah's witnesses insist that since the second occurrence of God/god in 1:1 is not preceded by the definite article (i.e. "the") in Greek, it should be translated as "a god" not God (the Greek article is often not translated into English). It is an indisputable fact, however, that the absence of the Greek article does not always mean the subject is indefinite—and that the Jehovah's Witness translators knew this is clear by the fact that there are at least fourteen places in the New World Translation of John's Gospel alone where the Greek word for God, *theos*, (θεος) appears without the Greek definite article and yet the Jehovah's Witnesses translators translate *theos* as definite anyway, i.e. as God with the capital G! In fact, there is only one other place in the entire Gospel of John (John 10:33) where they do not translate the word God with a small "g" when it appears without the article.
89   John 3:16; 6:40; 6:51; 6:54; 10:9.
90   John 8:58.

According to John 10:30 Jesus said, "I and my Father are one." Some have dismissed this simply as a oneness in mind and purpose, that is, the same kind of oneness that John 17:21 says Christians are supposed to have. In John 10:30, however, Jesus was claiming much more than just a oneness in mind and purpose. The writer of John clearly wanted readers to understand that Jesus was claiming oneness with God in a way that Jesus' Jewish audience considered blasphemous. In the words of Jesus' enemies, "It is not for a good work that we are going to stone you but for blasphemy, because you being a man, make yourself God." [91]

John clearly began his gospel proclaiming the deity of Jesus and he ended it the same way. In 20:24-29 "doubting Thomas" saw the risen Jesus and said to him, "My Lord and My God![92] It is important to note that Jesus did not rebuke Thomas for this worship but rather blessed him! There can be no serious doubt that the writer of John's Gospel wanted readers to understand that Jesus is the very incarnation of God!

---

91   John 10:31-34.
92   John 20:28.

Chapter Four

The Deity of the King
In the Rest of the New Testament

In Acts

In the Old Testament, salvation in a spiritual sense was only found in God but Acts 4:12, speaking of Jesus, says, "and there is salvation in no one else; for there is no other name under heaven that has been given among men by which we must be saved." In other words, the writer of Acts attributed to Jesus a power the Old Testament attributed to God alone. Acts 16:31 reinforces this by saying "Believe in the Lord Jesus and you will be saved." That which was only attributed to God in the Old Testament, is attributed to Jesus in the New Testament.

This is also true in Acts 2:21 where Peter quotes from Joel 2:32 which says that "...everyone who calls upon the name to the Lord [Yahweh] will be saved." Peter applies this quote directly to Jesus, i.e. everyone who calls on the name of Jesus will be saved. In other words, Peter took a quote which in its original context referred to Yahweh, and said that quote is referring to Jesus! Critics can disagree with Peter if they like, but it is pretty hard to deny that Peter was intending to attribute deity to Jesus.

In a Jewish culture, God was the final judge of the living and the dead but Acts 10:42 says that Jesus "is the One who has been appointed by God as judge of the living and dead." Once again, that which was attributed to God in the Old

Testament, in this case, final judgment, is attributed to Jesus in the New Testament.

In Paul's Letters

Paul is actually our very earliest witness to Jesus. As we saw in Acts, Paul also took the passage in Joel 2:32 which says that "...everyone who calls upon the name to the Lord [Yahweh] will be saved" and applied that directly to Jesus.[93] In other words, both Peter and Paul taught that we can be saved by calling on the name of Jesus, and as proof they cite Joel 2:32 which says that "everyone who calls on the name of Yahweh will be saved."

It is probable that Paul was also intending to directly attribute deity to Jesus in Romans 9:5 which could be translated, "from whom is Christ according to the flesh, who is God over all, blessed forever." Or, as the New Living Translation puts it, "Christ himself was a Jew as far as his human nature is concerned. *And he is God*, who rules over everything and is worthy of eternal praise" (emphasis mine).

In the Old Testament, it is through God that all things exist but according to Paul it is through Jesus that all things exist.[94] In Colossians, Paul repeats the teaching that creation comes through Jesus saying that it was by Jesus that "all things were created, both in heavens and on earth...."[95] As a good Rabbi, Paul knew full well that God is the only creator. That is why Paul wrote that Jesus "existed in the form of God"[96] and that "in Him the fullness of Deity dwells in bodily form."[97]

In Titus 2:13 Paul wrote, "Looking for the blessed hope and the appearing of the glory of our great God and Savior, Christ Jesus" (NAS). In Greek there is a way that Paul could

---

93   Romans 10:13, 17.
94   First Corinthians 8:6.
95   Colossians 1:16-17.
96   Philippians 2:6.
97   Colossians 2:9.

have distinguished between Father and Son in this passage, but the way he wrote this phrase in Greek makes it clear that he intended to call Jesus "our great God and Savior." [98]

In the General Epistles and Revelation

The Book of Hebrews refers to Jesus as the very "radiance of the glory of God and the exact imprint of his nature" and says that Jesus "upholds the universe by the word of his power".[99] The writer of Hebrews quotes from Psalm 2:7 to argue that God himself called Jesus his son.[100] Hebrews interprets Psalm 45:6-7 as saying that Yahweh said to Jesus "Your throne, O God, is forever and ever".[101] The author interpreted this Psalm to mean that Yahweh was calling Jesus, God. It is clear that the author of Hebrews intended to teach the deity of Jesus.

The deity of Jesus is also taught in First and Second Peter. First Peter 3:15 alludes to Isaiah 8:13 saying that *Jesus* is the one we should regard as holy! Isaiah 8:13 says "The LORD [Yahweh] of Hosts, him you shall regard as holy..." In other words, Peter took passage from Isaiah that referred to God and applied it directly to Jesus. Second Peter 1:1 speaks of "the righteousness of our God and Savior Jesus Christ." There is a way in Greek in which Peter could have made a distinction between our God, and our Savior Jesus Christ but Peter does not do this. In Greek it is clear that Peter intended to call Jesus, "Our God and Savior."

According to Revelation 22:13 Jesus said, "I am the alpha and omega, the first and the last, the beginning and the end," but "Revelation 1:8 said it was the Lord God who was

---

98   Most critics believe that Titus was written by a follower of Paul and not by Paul himself. I do not believe the critics are right but if they were it would provide even another example of first century AD belief in the deity of Jesus and would tend to confirm that we have not misunderstood Paul on this subject.

99   Hebrews 1:3.

100   Hebrews 1:5.

101   Hebrews 1:8.

the alpha and omega." What is particularly interesting about these passages is that they are also found in the Jehovah's Witness's *New World Translation* which goes to great lengths to remove any trace of Jesus' deity. They missed one. The *New World Translation* translates Revelation 1:8 as "I am the alpha and omega, says Jehovah God." But at the end of Revelation, the "alpha and omega" is the one who is coming quickly,[102] identified specifically as Jesus![103] Even the Jehovah's Witnesses own translation teaches the deity of Jesus!

It is no wonder, therefore, that Jesus was also the object of worship in the New Testament. Paul wrote that "at the name of Jesus every knee will bow."[104] Paul exclaimed that to Jesus "be glory forever and ever."[105] The author of Second Peter also proclaimed his worship for Jesus saying that to Jesus "be glory, both now and to the day of eternity."[106] Hebrews 1:6 says of Jesus, "let all the angels of God worship him." Revelation says that to Jesus "be the glory and dominion forever and ever"[107] and "To Him who sits on the throne, and to the Lamb [Jesus], be blessing and honor and dominion forever and ever...and the elders fell down and worshipped".[108] Remember that in a Jewish context only God was the object of worship!

102   Revelation 22:12-13.
103   Revelation 22:16. I once heard of a Jehovah's Witness who got saved precisely because a Christian was able to show her that her own Bible teaches that Jesus is God.
104   Philippians 2:10.
105   2 Timothy 4:18.
106   Second Peter 3:18.
107   Revelation 1:5-6.
108   Revelation 5:11-14.

Chapter Five

The Deity of the King
Outside the Bible

Is it possible that we have misunderstood what the New Testament teaches about Jesus' deity, as some cults would have us believe? Not a chance! Those who wrote shortly after the New Testament was written demonstrate conclusively that early Christians—including those who wrote the New Testament—absolutely believed that in Jesus, God had become flesh. For example, Clement of Rome, who wrote about AD 97, (about the time John wrote his Gospel and letters) described Jesus as the "radiance of God's majesty."[109] In about AD 110, Ignatius wrote about "our God, Jesus Christ"[110] and "Jesus Christ, our God,"[111] and "stirring up yourselves by the blood of God,[112] and "God Himself being manifested in human form"[113] and "I glorify God, even Jesus Christ,"[114] and "servants of Christ our God."[115]

The letter of Barnabas, written sometime between AD 70 and AD 135 (not the Barnabas of the Bible but some other Christian), says, "...the Son of God was the divine Lord, and the

109   Clement to the Corinthians, 16, 36. NB. Citations from the church fathers can be found in numerous sources, for example, Ehrman, Bart D. ed. *The Apostolic Fathers* (Loeb Classical Library). Cambridge, MA : Harvard University Press, 2003. Holmes, Michael, ed. *The Apostolic Fathers*. 3rd ed. Grand Rapids : Baker, 2007. Roberts, Alexander and James Donaldson, eds. *Ante-Nicene Fathers*. 10 volumes. Peabody, MA : Hendrickson, 1885, 1995.
110   Ignatius, to the Romans, 3; to the Ephesians, chapter 18.
111   Ignatius, to the Ephesians, Introduction.
112   Ignatius, to the Ephesians, chapter 1.
113   Ignatius, to the Ephesians, chapter 19.
114   Ignatius, to the Smyrneans, Introduction.
115   Ignatius, to the Smyrneans, chapter 10.

future Judge of living and dead alike."[116] The letter of Barnabas called Jesus "the Lord of all the earth," a title used in Joshua 3:13 to refer to God.[117] Justin Martyr, who died about AD 163, wrote that "...the Father of the universe has a Son; who also, being the first-begotten Word of God, is even God."[118]

The idea that Jesus was God is also found in ancient books known as the New Testament Apocrypha (not to be confused with the Apocrypha found in Catholic Bibles which was written before the time of Jesus). Most New Testament Apocrypha were written from the second to fourth or fifth centuries AD. One of these books is the Acts of Andrew (4th cent.) which says, "Andrew prayed thus: 'I pray you, my God, Lord Jesus Christ....'"

Another writing says, "O Jesus undefiled, we praise thee...we glorify thee; for thou art God alone".[119] The *Apocalypse of Peter* says, "... my Lord and God Jesus Christ".[120] The *"Acts of John"* says, "Glory be to thee, my Jesus, the only God of truth".[121] The *Acts of Thomas* says, "O God Jesus Christ, Son of the living God, redeemer...."[122] The *Ascension of Isaiah* says, "and he who gave permission is thy Lord, God, the Lord Christ, who will be called Jesus on earth."[123] In the Acts of Peter we find, "For this is the Lord and God of all, Jesus Christ whom I preach, and he is the Father of truth."[124] In the Acts of Paul and Thecla we find, "My God, Jesus Christ."[125]

The fact that these early Christians believed Jesus was God is also confirmed in secular sources. The Roman governor,

---

116   Barnabas Chapter 7
117   Barnabas 5:1.
118   First Apology of Justin LXIII. Note: an "apology" in this sense, is a "defense."
119   Acts of Peter 39.
120   Apocalypse of Peter, Ethiopic 16, 135 AD.
121   Acts of John 43, 2nd-3rd c.
122   Acts of Thomas 60, 3rd c.
123   Ascension of Isaiah 5, 2nd c.
124   Acts of Peter 26, 3rd c.
125   Acts of Paul and Thecla, 185-195 AD.

Pliny the Younger (AD 112), for example, conducted an investigation of Christians and reported to the Roman emperor that they "were in the habit of meeting on a certain fixed day before it was light, when they sang in alternative verses a hymn to Christ, as to a god."[126] Of course Pliny would write "to a god" instead of "to God" because Pliny didn't believe in just one God. Also in the early 100's AD, the anti-Christian satirist, Lucian also wrote of Christians saying that they "worship" Jesus.

In a once-popular novel called *The DaVinci Code*, the author wrote that no one before the fourth century AD believed that Jesus was God. That author couldn't have been more wrong! The point of all this is that the New Testament clearly teaches that Jesus is the God-King and that the very earliest Christians after New Testament times understood and believed this as well. These early Christians believed that the message of the Gospels and New Testament letters was the message of God.

---

126   Found in Pliny's letter to Emperor Trajan.

Chapter Six

The Resurrection of the King

Jesus, a Galilean carpenter as the God-King? How
on earth did Christianity even get off the ground with such
a notion? Why would anyone believe such a thing about an
ordinary Galilean carpenter like Jesus? It is important to note
that many people did not believe it. Some thought Jesus
was a blasphemer.[127] Some thought he was crazy or demon
possessed.[128] That is precisely what we might expect people
to think of an ordinary carpenter who proclaimed himself to
be King. The question is, why would *anyone* believe that this
Galilean was their long awaited Messiah/King?

Jesus' followers undoubtedly had a number of reasons
for believing, but there seem to be three primary ones.
First, they were convinced that Jesus had genuinely fulfilled
prophecies about the coming King. The Gospel of Matthew,
in particular, goes to some length to show that Jesus was the
fulfillment of prophecies about the coming of the Christ-King.
It is most likely that Matthew wrote about these prophecies
because that is what the earliest Christians genuinely believed
about Jesus.

Second, Jesus' followers believed him because they
were convinced that he had done genuine miracles. We have
no record of anyone in the ancient world denying that Jesus
was a wonder-worker. Even first century Jewish historian,
Josephus, confirms that Jesus did amazing works. Jesus'
enemies tried to dismiss his miracles as magic tricks or the

---

127   John 10:33.
128   John 10:20.

work of Satan, but no one denied that he did them. Jesus' followers were, of course, aware of Jewish magicians and other wonder-workers but according to the Gospels they said that no one has ever done anything like this before.[129]

Finally, Jesus' followers were absolutely convinced that Jesus had physically come back to life again after being dead. Many people today, of course, find this hard to accept. After all, people just don't come back to life after having been dead for "three days." They may argue that this is the kind of superstition that may have been accepted by people in ancient times, but in the modern age we just know better. Besides, they argue, there are plenty of explanations for what could have happened to the body of Jesus. Perhaps it was stolen. Perhaps Jesus' disciples saw a hallucination of the "risen Jesus." Maybe Jesus didn't actually die, so when his disciples saw him after his crucifixion they just assumed that he had risen. Maybe the whole story was just fabricated based on earlier popular Middle Eastern stories of dying and rising savior gods. Besides, if Jesus had really risen, wouldn't we expect that it would have received wider attention than just in four Christian Gospels?

With so many objections, how could any intelligent person still believe in the resurrection of Jesus? We could be cynical and say the key word is "intelligent" but the fact is that there are many people with Ph.D.s who believe Jesus rose from the dead. What reasons could they possibly have?

First, virtually all historians and New Testament scholars agree that the Romans executed Jesus by crucifixion. Crucifixion was considered to be a very shameful way to die. The Jewish Torah even taught that someone dying in this manner was cursed! Most biblical scholars don't believe that early Christians would make up a story about their Messiah

---

129   Cf. John 3:2; 9:32; 15:24.

being shamefully executed in a manner indicating that he was a cursed criminal. This is because such a story would be an embarrassment which would hinder the spread of their message. Because of this, and the fact that Jesus' crucifixion is confirmed even by ancient non-Christian sources—like Josephus, Tacitus, Lucian of Samosata and Mara Bar-Serapion[130]—Jesus' crucifixion is recognized as a fact of history by virtually all biblical scholars whether they believe in the resurrection or not.

Second, the tomb of Jesus was found empty. The four biblical Gospels (all written in the first century when Jesus was crucified) specifically claim that Jesus' tomb was empty, as does the second century "*Gospel of Peter*. Regardless of one's view on this, there can be little reasonable doubt that the Gospels are windows into what first century Christians *believed* about Jesus, and early Christians clearly believed the tomb was empty.

Even the most skeptical of scholars believe that the Gospels contain *some* historical information,[131] and most biblical scholars—even those who do not believe in the resurrection—believe the story of the empty tomb is one of those reliable pieces of information. One reason that even skeptical scholars believe the tomb was empty is that the Gospel writers are unanimous in presenting women as the first eyewitnesses to the empty tomb. In the ancient Jewish and Greco-Roman world, women were not considered reliable witnesses. If the story of the risen Jesus was just fiction, we have to ask why the Gospel writers would try to persuade people to believe a fictional story by saying that the story

---

130   For a discussion of these, and other ancient sources for Jesus see Gary R. Habermas. *The Historical Jesus; Ancient Evidence for the Life of Christ*. (College Press, 1996). Robert Van Voorst. *Jesus Outside the New Testament*. (Grand Rapids : Eerdmans, 2000).
131   See Lee Martin McDonald, *The Story of Jesus in History and Faith*. (Grand Rapids : Baker, 2013), 334-336) for a list of solidly established facts that can be known about Jesus purely as matters of history.

was supported by people whom their culture considered to be unreliable. As a modern example, if you were making up a story to convince people that President Kennedy had risen from the dead, would you try to prove your point by saying that alcoholics or drug abusers were the first eyewitnesses? Of course not! Even many skeptical scholars are convinced, therefore, that for whatever reason, the tomb of Jesus was found to be empty after he had been buried in it.

Those same stories that convince even skeptical scholars that the tomb was empty, however, also say that the women spoke with and even touched the risen Jesus. Why would skeptics accept the evidence that points to the empty tomb, but reject the very same evidence when it points to the risen Jesus? Their reasoning has little to do with historical evidence and everything to do with a philosophical bias against the possibility of resurrection.

The earliest explanation for the empty tomb is found in the Gospel of Matthew which says the soldiers who had guarded the tomb reported that the body was stolen while they slept. The soldiers were obviously lying: if they were really sleeping, how could they possibly know what happened? If early skeptics believed, however, that someone must have stolen the body, it would be an admission even by these skeptics that the tomb was indeed empty. Even if the stolen body explanation was judged to be plausible, however, we would still have to account for the stories that say Jesus was seen physically alive after his death.

A few writers have suggested that Jesus survived the crucifixion, then somehow got out of the tomb and managed to convince his disciples that he was their risen Messiah. This is unlikely to say the least. Three crucified friends of Josephus (a first century Jewish historian) were taken off their crosses after just a few hours. Although all of them presumably received medical attention, two of them died the same day, and the third one died shortly thereafter. It takes a lot of faith, therefore, to believe the idea that although Jesus had been scourged, was crucified for several hours, and then left in a tomb without medical attention, he somehow managed to survive and get out of the tomb.

An article in the *Journal of the American Medical Association*[132] examines Jesus' death, in graphic detail, from a medical perspective in light of what we know about Roman crucifixion. Actual crucifixion was often even more brutal than the portrayal in Mel Gibson's "The Passion of the Christ"! The authors of the JAMA article demonstrate how unrealistic it is to think that Jesus survived his treatment by the Romans, especially in a culture that lacked modern medicine.

But let's suspend all reality for a moment and assume that Jesus somehow managed to survive the crucifixion. He would then have to get out of a dark tomb (which would involve moving a rock large enough that it would likely have taken several healthy men to move), and then walk or crawl to his disciples. They would have undoubtedly been shocked that Jesus survived. They may have even seen his survival as a miracle of God, but it is rather absurd to think that anyone would have hailed this very bloody, bruised and broken man (most likely in serious or critical condition) as their resurrected Lord and Savior!

Third, Jesus was believed to have appeared alive *physically* after his execution. Matthew, for example, records that the women who met the resurrected Jesus "took hold of his feet and worshipped him." According to the Gospel of Luke, Jesus met with the disciples after his resurrection and said, "See my hands and feet, that it is I myself. Touch me, and see. For a spirit does not have flesh and bones as you see that

---

132   March 21, 1986.

I have." Luke then records that the risen Jesus ate fish with his disciples. According to the Gospel of John, the risen Jesus had to tell Mary Magdalene—one of the women who found the tomb empty—to stop clinging or holding on to him! The same Gospel records that Jesus later invited Thomas to touch the marks left by the nails and spear.

Regardless of whether critics believe these stories, it is beyond legitimate dispute that the Gospel writers intended to communicate that the resurrection of Jesus *was physical*, not merely "spiritual." It also seems to be beyond reasonable doubt that in the Gospels we are in touch with what early Christians believed happened to Jesus—and they were convinced that Jesus physically rose from the dead. That we have not misunderstood the Gospels on this point is clear from the writings of Ignatius who wrote shortly after the last New Testament book was written saying that Jesus was still in the flesh even after his resurrection.[133]

Even before the Gospels were written, however, the apostle Paul strongly affirmed the physical resurrection of Jesus in a letter we now call "First Corinthians." Regardless of whether critics believe this letter to be inspired Scripture or not, even the most skeptical scholars believe that Paul wrote this letter about AD 56. In First Corinthians Paul wrote that Jesus was raised on the third day and that he was seen by James, and by Jesus' disciples, and by more than 500 others. It seems pretty clear that Paul was not intending to say 500 people had hallucinations or visions! Not only that, but Paul used the word "resurrection" to describe what happened to

---

133   Ignatius to the Smyrneans, 3. It is important to note, however, that Jesus' resurrection was more than just the resuscitation of a dead body. As McDonald points out, "Jesus' new mode of existence was bodily, but not limited by the physical realm of this-worldly existence." According to the Gospels, Jesus' resurrected body, though flesh and bones, could apparently appear or disappear and pass through walls (for the quote and discussion see Lee Martin McDonald, *The Story of Jesus in History and Faith*. (Grand Rapids : Baker), 325-328).

Jesus. In his book, *The Resurrection of the Son of God,*[134] N.T. Wright conclusively demonstrated that in Paul's time the word "resurrection" meant the body came back to life. It never meant that the spirit lived on after death which is something most people believed anyway.

Paul argued that his entire message and ministry rises or falls on the resurrection of Jesus. If Jesus did not rise from the dead, Paul says, "our preaching is in vain and your faith is in vain...and you are still in your sins." In the letter we know as Second Corinthians, Paul reminded his readers of the problems he had faced for preaching the gospel, including hunger, thirst, imprisonment, whippings, beatings and life-threatening dangers like being stoned (with real stones)! Yet so convinced was he that Jesus actually came back to life Paul he would let nothing stop him!

From all we know about other early Christians, they too were so convinced Jesus had risen from the dead that they were willing to face prison, torture and even death to proclaim that fact. It is important to note that they weren't dying just for a good cause (Many people have died for a good cause) and they weren't dying just for their message of love and compassion (Their fellow Jews also preached love and compassion). Jesus' followers were willing to face enormous suffering because they were convinced that Jesus had come back to life. This fact, among others, convinced them that Jesus really was who he claimed to be—who the Gospels claimed him to be.

Fourth, belief in the resurrection of Jesus was widespread. In the first century, all four biblical gospels and Acts, Paul's letters, First Peter, the Book of Revelation and a letter written by Clement of Rome all claim that Jesus rose

---

134   Wright, N.T. *The Resurrection of the Son of God*. (Minneapolis : Fortress Press, 2003).

from the dead. In the second century, the resurrection of
Jesus is affirmed by Ignatius, Polycarp, the *Didache*, the *Epistle
of Barnabas*, *The Shepherd of Hermas*, Papias, the *Epistle of
Diognetus*, Irenaeus, Justin Martyr, Tertullian, Athenagoras,
Theophilus, Minucius Felix, Hippolytus, Origen, and Tatian.[135]
Even some of the so-called "lost gospels" from the second or
third centuries affirm Jesus' resurrection, for example, *The
Gospel of Peter*, *The Acts of Peter*, *The Gospel of Philip*, *The
Gospel of the Savior*, *The Apocryphon of James*, the *Treatise on
the Resurrection*, and others.[136] The fact is that there are more
sources that affirm the resurrection of Jesus written within
150 years of his death than there are to affirm the *existence* of
Tiberius Caesar within 150 years of his death!

One of the critic's own criteria for determining if
something actually happened is called "Multiple Independent
Attestation." This criteria says that if an event is recorded
in multiple independent sources we have more reason to
believe that it actually happened. The physical resurrection of
Jesus is recorded in multiple independent sources—even the
critics would acknowledge Mark and John, for example, to be
independent sources—and yet the critics deny it happened.
Their denial is not based on lack of historical evidence, but on
a philosophical bias (i.e. a closed mind) against the possibility
of resurrection.

Finally, based on the considerations above we could
treat the resurrection of Jesus as a historical hypothesis. The
strength of any hypothesis is its explanatory power. In other
words, a good hypothesis will explain the data. As it turns out,
the hypothesis that Jesus rose from the dead explains a lot
that is difficult to explain otherwise.

---

135   All of these church fathers can be found in Roberts, Alexander and James
Donaldson, eds. *Ante-Nicene Fathers*. 10 volumes. Peabody, MA : Hendrickson, 1885, 1995.
136   These so-called "lost gospels" can be found in Robinson, James M. *The Nag
Hammadi Library*. Rev. ed. San Francisco : HarperSanFrancisco, 1988.

First, the hypothesis of Jesus' resurrection explains the conversion of Paul. By his own testimony (in letters that even the most skeptical of scholars consider genuine) Paul violently opposed Christianity—even to the point of imprisoning and killing Christians.[137] This testimony by Paul is also supported by Luke. How did someone like Paul go from being such a rabid opponent of Christianity to one of its most ardent promoters? Paul himself would say the change was due to his conviction that Jesus had risen from the dead.

Second, the hypothesis of Jesus' resurrection explains the conversion of Jesus' half-brother James. The first century Jewish historian, Josephus, describes James as a very pious Jew. According to the Gospels, James didn't even believe in Jesus at first.[138] But James became one of the leaders of the early church. The resurrection of Jesus is a very probable explanation for this radical change in his thinking.

Third, the hypothesis of Jesus' resurrection explains the change in worship from the Sabbath (Saturday) to the first day of the week (Sunday). For first-century Jews, observance of the Sabbath was a huge deal! Some scholars have called it one of the "boundary markers" that identified them as faithful Jews. By Paul's time, Jews had worshipped on the Sabbath for hundreds of years and the Torah prescribed serious consequences for violating the Sabbath. For Jewish Christians (and all of the very earliest Christians were Jews) to change the day of worship from the Sabbath to Sunday was not like a church today deciding to add a Saturday night worship service. It would be more analogous to PETA suddenly deciding to sponsor animal sacrifices of puppies! A monumental change like that always demands an explanation. So it is with worship on Sunday. The fact that early Christians were convinced that

---

137   Galatians 1:13; First Corinthians 15:9; Acts 7:59-8:3; 9:1-5; 22:4-14; 26:12-20.
138   John 7:5.

Jesus rose from the dead on the first day of the week (Sunday) would be sufficient to explain the change.

Fourth, the hypothesis of Jesus' resurrection explains the continuation of the Jesus movement even after his death. Jesus was not the only man in the ancient world believed to be the Jewish "Messiah." While ancient Jews had different ideas about what their "Messiah" would be like, most seemed to expect a military leader who would forcibly kick the Romans out of Judea. When the Romans crushed these Messiah wannabes, their movements always died along with them. The thinking was that the true Messiah would kick out the oppressive Romans, so any would-be-Messiah who was crushed by the Romans could not possibly be the true Messiah! What could possibly explain why the Jesus movement alone would continue after their "Messiah" had been brutally executed by the Romans? Belief in the resurrection of Jesus would be a plausible explanation.

Fifth, although many first century Jews believed in a physical resurrection of the dead at the final judgment, no one, as far as we can tell, believed in a physical resurrection (not just resuscitation as for example the story of Elijah raising the dead[139]) of human beings before that time (Mythical stories of gods dying and rising after the pattern of the rising and setting sun, or the Winter/Spring crop cycles are no exception). In fact, Paul was even mocked for preaching such a crazy idea.[140] The reason first century Christians preached that someone had actually been resurrected before the final judgment is that they were genuinely convinced that it happened to Jesus.

Finally, the hypothesis of Jesus' resurrection explains why early Christians began worshiping Jesus and equating him

---

139   1 Kings 17:7-24. In a resuscitation the person raised, like Lazarus, would eventually die again. A resurrected person receives a physical but imperishable body that will never die.
140   Acts 17:32.

with God (see above on Jesus' deity). The fact that we have not misunderstood the New Testament on this is confirmed both by Christian and non-Christian sources in the second century. The Christian, Ignatius, for example, is very clear that Jesus was worshipped as God. Non-Christians like Pliny the Younger and Lucian also confirm that Christians worshipped Jesus as a god. For first century Jews, the fact that there was one and only one God was absolutely foundational. Something must account for the fact that these early Christians (and remember, all of the earliest Christians were Jewish) started worshipping Jesus as God, a practice which has continued since the first century. The resurrection of Jesus would account for such a change.

Interestingly enough, the resurrection by itself would not cause someone to believe Jesus as God or a god. As N.T. Wright explained,[141] for someone to have come back from the dead might lead people to believe that the world was a much stranger place than they once imagined, but it would not, by itself, lead anyone to believe such a person was a god. However, if Jesus had taught his disciples the kinds of things the Gospels say he taught them, for example, that he and the Father are one,[142] the resurrection would explain why they would believe such a thing and began to worship him.

Of course we've barely scratched the surface when it comes to arguments about the resurrection of Jesus. For much more thorough and scholarly discussions, see *The Resurrection of the Son of God* by N.T. Wright (817 pages)[143] and *The Resurrection of Jesus* by Michael R. Licona (718 pages)![144] Or for a shorter, easier to understand perspective,

---

141   N.T. Wright. *New Testament and the People of God.* (Minneapolis : Fortress Press).
142   John 10:30-33.
143   Wright, N.T. *The Resurrection of the Son of God.* (Minneapolis : Fortress Press, 2003).
144   Licona, *Michael R. The Resurrection of Jesus; A New Historiographical Approach.* (Downers Grove, IL : IVP, 2010).

see *The Case for the Resurrection* by Gary Habermas and
Michael Licona (384 pages).[145] Evidence like that presented
above has convinced even many highly skeptical scholars
that it is historical fact that Jesus' earliest followers sincerely
believed he had risen from the dead. These skeptical scholars
are quick to add, however, that we can be certain that Jesus
didn't actually rise from the dead because dead people just
don't come back to life. In other words, their position is based
on a philosophical conviction (faith) that God either does not
exist, or if God does exist, God would never, ever, under any
circumstances, intervene in human events in ways that would
look supernatural to us—like a resurrection.

I understand why atheists must believe (in spite of how
strong the evidence is) that no dead person could possibly
ever come back to life. What seems rather inconsistent,
however, is the position of some ministers in mainline
churches who claim to believe in a God powerful enough
to create the universe, but who confidently assert that God
would not or could not ever raise the dead. In light of the
evidence, how can they possibly be so dogmatic about what a
creator-God could not or would not do?

In the final analysis, nothing can be "proven" beyond
all possible doubt. There is always a gap that can be crossed
only by faith (this is also true in science, by the way). Those
of us who have examined the evidence, however, and have
experienced what we believe to be the grace and power of
God in our lives, and the witness of the Spirit in our hearts,
have no trouble proclaiming with Christians around the world
that He is risen indeed!

---

145   Habermas, Gary and Michael Licona. *The Case for the Resurrection of Jesus.* (Grand
Rapids : Kregel, 2004).

Conclusion to Part One

Part one has argued that the idea that Jesus is not only the Christ, the King of kings and Lord of lords, [146] but also the very incarnation of God[147] is not something drawn from a few isolated proof-texts, but is a major theme throughout the New Testament. The New Testament claims that Jesus is the Creator-King are substantiated by, among other things, substantial historical evidence for the resurrection. The point of all this discussion is that according to the New Testament, Jesus is not our co-pilot. He is not our spiritual advisor. He is not some kind of genie who exists to grant us our every wish. He is our Creator-King to whom we owe absolute devotion, allegiance and service.[148] This is the subject of Part two.

---

146   For more extensive development of this theme in the Gospels, see N.T. Wright, *How God became King.* (New York : HarperOne, 2012).

147   For a much more thoroughly and scholarly discussion of the deity of Jesus in the New Testament, see Murray Harris, *Jesus as God; the New Testament Use of Theos in Reference to Jesus.* (Wipf & Stock Pub., 2008).

148   How does this absolute lordship of Jesus relate to our citizenship in America or any other country? Jewish zealots or Siccari in first century Judea, whose battle cry was "no Lord but God," sought to overturn pagan rule by force. Jesus would have none of that! If we would be good followers of Jesus, we would be, as much as possible, model citizens of the countries in which we live (Mark 12:17 || Matthew 22:21 || Luke 20:25; Matthew 17:27; Romans 13:1-7; 1 Peter 2:13-17). If our government were to command us, however, do things that the Bible forbids (e.g. commit murder by performing abortions) or to refrain from doing things the Bible commands (e.g. evangelizing), then we must obey God rather than man regardless of the consequences (Acts 5:27-29).

PART II
SERVING THE KING

Chapter Seven

The Demands of the King

One of the few things that Evangelicals and critics agree upon is that one of the major topics of Jesus' preaching was the Kingdom of God. What the critics often miss, however, is that Jesus not only taught about the Kingdom of God, he presented himself as the king of that kingdom. It is in light of Jesus' kingship and deity that his demands for allegiance must be understood. Make no mistake about it, Jesus as God-King demands absolute allegiance.

For example, according to all four Gospels, Jesus taught that his followers must be willing to sacrifice their own lives for him if called upon to do so. According to Mark, for example, Jesus said,

> If any man would come after me, let him deny himself and take up his cross and follow me. For whoever would save his life will lose it; and whoever loses his life for my sake and the gospel's will safe it, for what does it profit a man to gain the whole world and forfeit his life" [soul].[149]

Similarly, in John 12:25 Jesus said, "Whoever loves his life loses it, and whoever hates his life in this world will keep it for eternal life."

When someone joins the military they may be called upon to go anywhere, face enormous hardships and even to sacrifice their own lives out of love for and service to their country. It shouldn't be so surprising that our King would ask for the same allegiance even unto death. In Revelation 2:10 Jesus told the church at Smyrna,

149   Mark 8:34-36//Matt 16:24-26//Luke 9:23-25.

> Do not be afraid of what you are about to suffer.
> I tell you, the devil will put some of you in prison
> to test you, and you will suffer persecution for ten
> days.[150] *Be faithful, even to the point of death*, and
> I will give you the crown of life.[151]

In Revelation 2:12-13 Jesus commended the church at Pergamum for remaining faithful to him and not renouncing their faith even after a faithful witness in their church was executed for his faith in Jesus. In Revelation 12:11 the writer commended those who "overcame" Satan "by the blood of the Lamb and by the word of their testimony" and "did not love their lives so much as to shrink from death." In other words, they chose to die rather than to deny Jesus.

Similarly, in Hebrews 11:35-38 the author wrote of Old Testament saints who were "tortured and refused to be released, so they might gain a better resurrection." He wrote that some "faced jeers and flogging, while others were chained and put in prison. They were stoned; they were sawed in two; they were put to death by the sword." The writer of Hebrews was making the point that his readers should follow the example of these Old Testament heroes if called upon to do so. In other words, we should love Jesus our King even more than we love our own life!

In fact, Jesus called us to love him even more than we love the most precious people in our lives:

> "He who loves father or mother more than me is
> not worthy of me; and he who loves son or daugh-
> ter more than me is not worthy of me; and he
> who does not take his cross and follow me is not
> worthy of me. He who finds his life will lose it, and
> he who loses his life for my sake will find it.[152]

Most of us love our father, mother, sons and daughters even more than we love our own life! It should be noted that

---

150   A symbolic number, probably denoting completion.
151   Revelation 2:10.
152   Matthew 10:37-39, cf. Luke 14:25-27; 17:33; John 12:25.

this is absolutely 180 degrees opposite of what Mark Shaw described in his discussion of America's return to "spirituality":

> What kind of spirituality are the returning prodigals discovering?...the new pilgrims seem to have post-Christian appetites. New Age spirituality, selfist spirituality, pantheistic mysticism and other forms of self-absorbed pseudopiety seem to appeal to many of the new seekers. The real object of their worship seems to be themselves.[153]

In other words, while many Americans consider themselves religious or spiritual in some respect, their "religion" is often a self-centered religion, tailor-made to their own liking. For many—even some who call themselves Christian—their religion allows them to imagine that Jesus would support pretty much any lifestyle they choose. Do they want to leave their husband or wife because they found someone they want more? No problem. They think Jesus will understand. Do they regularly lie, cheat, steal, get drunk or behave immorally? No problem. Jesus loves them no matter what they do—or so they imagine. They are the center of their little religious universe and their image of Jesus is no more real than the family idol a Hindu may put on a shelf.

By contrast, the Jesus of the Bible calls followers to value him more than our own life and even more than the most beloved people in our lives! Although this may sound extreme—and it is—Dallas Seminary professor Howard Hendricks once put it in perspective by pointing out that for Christians, this love provides the anchor that holds everything in place. Hendricks said, "Husbands, you will never love your wife as Christ loved the Church until Jesus is the absolute lord of your life."[154] Loving Jesus above all else is sometimes the

---

153   Mark Shaw. *Great Ideas from Church History*. (Downers Grove, IL : IVP Press, 1997). Although written over a decade ago, his comments still seem to be just a relevant today.

154   I'm quoting this from memory of a cassette tape of a lesson taught by Dr. Hendricks many years ago. His teaching, like that of Jesus, was often unforgettable.

only anchor you have left when loved ones forsake you or turn against you and your world starts falling apart. Loving Jesus above all else enables you to show love to others when they are absolutely unlovable.

Many modern "Christians" seem to think that "Christianity" is almost solely about being compassionate and nice to people. As important as compassion is, New Testament Christianity is about much more than compassion. All too many "Christians" seem to believe in a kind of all-tolerant, non-judgmental Jesus who excuses sin and exists as some kind of cosmic Santa Claus or vending machine to grant our requests. This Jesus is a modern myth. The Gospels definitely paint a different picture.

According to the Gospels, Jesus was a fiery preacher who warned of judgment and called for repentance.[155] Jesus warned that it is better to go through life maimed than to be thrown with two hands, feet and eyes into hell where the "worm does not die, and the fire is not quenched."[156] In both Matthew and Luke[157] Jesus warned people not to fear those who could kill the body, but rather to "fear him who can destroy both soul and body in hell."[158] Jesus told scribes and Pharisees they would receive "greater condemnation" for their hypocritical show of piety.[159] He told a parable about the owner of a vineyard who would deal with his rebellious tenants by destroying them and giving the vineyard to others.[160]

---

155   Mark 1:14; Matthew 4:17; Lk 3:3.
156   Mark 9:43-48 // Matthew 5:28-30; 18:8-9. This phrase is a quote from Isaiah 66:24 and metaphorically refers to eternal judgment in which the maggots (worms) never stop feeding and the fire never goes out.
157   Passages often attributed to "the sayings source, Q" which is a hypothetical source that many scholars believe was used by the authors of Matthew and Luke in the composition of their Gospels. The significance is that many critics seem to give even more credence to "Q" than they do the four Gospels.
158   Matthew 10:28 // Luke 12:4-5.
159   Matthew 23:14 // Mark 12:40 // Luke 20:47.
160   Matthew 12:8-9 // Luke 20:15 // Matthew 21:41.

Jesus said that Capernaum would be brought down to Hades[161] and in a parable about a faithful and unfaithful servant, Jesus warned that the servant's master would come unexpectedly and punish him with the hypocrites where "men will weep and gnash their teeth."[162] Jesus' parable of the talents ends with the worthless servant being cast into outer darkness where "men will weep and gnash their teeth."[163] Jesus point in the parable of the minas[164] is similar to his teaching in the parable of the talents.

Matthew's unique material[165] is even more shocking. Jesus warned that "the sons of the kingdom would be thrown into outer darkness" where people would "weep and gnash their teeth."[166] In fact, Jesus said it would "be more tolerable on the day of judgment for the land of Sodom and Gomorrah" than for the town that rejects his message.[167] Speaking of the judgment at the end of the age, Jesus warned that the angels would "gather out of his kingdom all causes of sin and all evildoers, and throw them into the furnace of fire; there men will weep and gnash their teeth."[168] At the final judgment Jesus will separate the "sheep" from the "goats" sending the latter into "the eternal fire prepared for the devil and his angels."[169] In Matthew 23 Jesus absolutely unloaded on the religious leaders of his generation calling them hypocrites, blind guides, whitewashed tombs, greedy self-indulgent fools and children of hell![170]

---

161   Matthew 11:21-24 // Luke 10:12-15.
162   Matthew 24:50-51 // Luke 12:46.
163   Matthew 25:14-3. The "talents" in this passage are not special abilities like musical talent. A talent was a weight of silver or gold.
164   Luke 19:11-27. A mina was a small coin.
165   When scholars write about Matthew's unique material, they are talking about passages in Matthew that are found only in Matthew, not Mark, Luke or John. In other words, it is not material that Matthew borrowed from Mark. It is, in this case, independent historical confirmation that Jesus really was sometimes a fiery preacher of judgment and repentance.
166   Matthew 8:12.
167   Matthew 10:18.
168   Matthew 13:42, cf. 49-50 and 22:13.
169   Matthew 25:41, cf. 46.
170   Matthew 23:15-17; cf. Luke 11:42-44.

In passages unique to Luke Jesus said that the unfaithful servant who knew his master's will but did not act accordingly, would receive a "severe beating."[171] The point seems to be that the eternal punishment will be more severe for those who knew God's word and deliberately ignored or rejected it.

Jesus warned his audience that unless they repent, they would perish like those Galileans who were slaughtered by Herod or like those who died when the tower of Siloam fell.[172] Jesus warned his Jewish audience that one day workers of evil would find themselves shut out and be ordered to depart to a place where they would weep and gnash their teeth.[173] In his parable of the Great Banquet, Jesus warned that none of those invited would taste of the banquet.[174] Finally, Jesus told a story about a rich man who died, was buried and was in anguish and torment in the flames of Hades.[175]

The judgmental tone of Jesus' message recorded in the Synoptic Gospels (Matthew, Mark and Luke) is also found in the Gospel of John where Jesus is recorded as saying that those who do not believe in him are "condemned already" since they "loved darkness rather than light, because their deeds were evil."[176] Jesus spoke of those who have done evil coming out of the tombs to "resurrection of judgment."[177] He reportedly told his antagonists that it was Moses who would be their accuser.[178] Jesus called his contemporaries liars who did not know God and he charged that the devil, not God, was

---

171   Luke 12:47.
172   Luke 13:5.
173   Luke 13:28.
174   Luke 14:24, cf. Matthew 22:13.
175   Luke 16:22-24.
176   John 3:18-19.
177   John 5:28-29.
178   John 5:38-45.

their father.[179] Jesus said they would die in their sin.[180]

It is important to note that Jesus attacked not just the Jewish leaders, but his entire *generation* for their condemnation of both John and Jesus.[181] In John's gospel Jesus proclaimed that "*Everyone* who does evil hates the light."[182] Jesus declared that it was *the world*—not just religious leaders—that hate him because he testified "that what it does is evil."[183] John would have us understand that in the middle of the feast of booths, Jesus stood up and told everyone "not one of you keeps the law."[184]

According to Mark, Jesus addressed *anyone*—not just religious leaders—who would be ashamed of him in what he calls, "this adulterous and sinful generation." [185] Jesus called his generation a faithless generation.[186] In Matthew Jesus called it an evil generation[187] and warned that "the sons of the kingdom"—not just religious leaders—"would be thrown into outer darkness" where people would "weep and gnash their teeth."[188] In Luke Jesus predicted that he would be rejected—not just by the Jewish leadership—but by "this generation."[189] In passages attributed to Q, Jesus spoke of an "evil generation" that asks for a sign.[190] At the final judgment even the inhabitants of Tyre and Sidon will rise up and condemn the Jewish villages that rejected Jesus.[191] In fact, Jesus apparently

---

179   John 8:19, 42-44, 55.
180   John 8:21.
181   Luke 7:31-35//Mt 11:16-19.
182   John 3:20.
183   John 7:7; 15:18, cf. 17:14.
184   John 7:19.
185   Mark 8:38. Parallels in Matthew and Luke leave out the adulterous part (Mark 8:38//Matthew 16:26//Luke 9:26).
186   Parallels in both Matthew and Luke read "faithless and perverse generation" (Mark 9:19/Matthew 17:17//Luke 9:41) and seemed to express exasperation with them asking, "how long shall I put up with you?" (Mark 9:19 // Matthew 17:17 // Luke 9:41).
187   Matthew 12:45.
188   Matthew 8:12.
189   Luke 17:25.
190   Luke 11:29//Mt:12:39; 16:4. Matthew adds "adulterous."
191   Luke 10:13-15 // Mt 11:20-24.Also in Q, when Jesus sends his disciples out into

considered his generation so evil that even the Gentiles of Nineveh and the Queen of the South would one day condemn it.[192]

Many have argued that statements like these are evidence of the anti-Semitic[193] nature of the early church rather than the genuine teaching of Jesus. This seems to ignore that fact that this kind of strong Jewish self-critique[194] attributed to Jesus in the Gospels—far from being anti-Semitic—is actually characteristic of ancient Judaism. For example, the Torah portrays the Children of Israel as rebellious and hard-hearted, a "crooked and twisted generation," a "foolish and senseless people" who are "no longer his children."[195] Similarly, Isaiah calls the people of Judah "offspring of evildoers," a "sinful nation" who are "laden with iniquity."[196] He even calls Jerusalem the city that "has become a whore."[197] Jeremiah accuses both Israel and Judah of being a "foolish and senseless people"[198] who have "stubborn and rebellious" hearts.[199] Hosea says "There is no faithfulness of steadfast love, and no knowledge of God in the land" but rather "there is swearing, lying, murder, stealing, and committing adultery...."[200]

Examples from the prophets could literally go on for pages. The point is that the writings in the New Testament are

---

the villages he warns them, "Go! I am sending you out like lambs among wolves..." (Luke 10:3// Matthew 10:16). In yet another Q passage, Jesus is probably not just thinking of religious leaders when he condemns sinners in general saying, "I never knew you. Away from me you evildoers" (Luke 6:27-28//Matthew. 7:23-24).

192   Luke 11:31-32//Matthew 12:42, 41.
193   i.e. anti-Jewish.
194   It is important to bear in mind that the supposed "anti-Semitic" criticism found in the New Testament is not an expression of Gentile criticism against Jews, but of Jewish self-criticism!
195   e.g. Exodus 15:24; 16:2-3; 17:2-4; Leviticus 26:41; Numbers 14:1-44; 20:3-5; Deuteronomy 31:15-18; 32:5-6.
196   Isaiah 1:4.
197   Isaiah 1:21.
198   Jeremiah 5:21.
199   Jeremiah 5:23.
200   Hosea 4:1-2.

not anti-Semitic. They are characteristic of Jewish self-critique and there is good historical reason to believe that Jesus' condemnation of his generation goes back to Jesus himself and was not invented by the early church as many critics like to insist.[201] Like Jewish prophets and writers before and after him, Jesus found it necessary to strongly condemn the sinfulness of his generation, to warn them of coming judgment, and to call his entire generation—not just the religious leaders or individual groups—to repentance.

The fact is there was apparently much within Jesus' contemporary Jewish culture with which he was not pleased—and if he was not pleased with his relatively moral Jewish culture, we can only shudder at what he must think of our immoral and godless culture in which most people own Bibles and there are churches in virtually every town! How much more would he not be pleased with those call themselves Christian but who are more concerned with entertainment and prosperity than they are with the pleasing God. The point of this discussion on sin is not just to stack up a pile of guilt (many people already live with enough guilt to crush an elephant!) but to force us to our knees before the cross of Christ in total dependence on his grace! This begins with repentance.

---

201   This would be supported by the criteria of multiple independent attestation.

Chapter Eight

Repentance, and Faith in the King

In light of Jesus' assessment of his culture it should not be surprising that over and over again, our King called his generation—and by implication, ours—to repentance. He came preaching, "Repent, for the Kingdom of God is at hand." In fact, the very first words of Jesus' public ministry recorded by Matthew and Mark are a call to repentance.[202] Later, when Jesus sent out his apostles to preach the Kingdom of God, "they went out and preached that men should repent."[203] Jesus told people that if they did not repent they would perish just like those whom Pilate had slaughtered or who died when the tower of Siloam fell on them.[204] Jesus' parables of the lost sheep, the lost coin, and the prodigal son all make the point that "there will be more rejoicing in heaven over one sinner who repents than over ninety-nine righteous persons who do not need to repent."[205] Jesus' story about the rich man and Lazarus is about the final torment of those who will not repent.[206]

Of what was this evil generation to repent? Their sin, of course. Although some people seem to act as though Jesus never spoke of sin, the fact is that he gave pretty comprehensive summary of sin noting that sin does not consist of outward actions alone, but begins in the heart:

---

202   Matthew 4:17; Mark 1:15.
203   Mark 6:6-13; Matthew 10:1-14; Luke 9:1-6.
204   Luke 13:1-5.
205   Luke 15:4-32.
206   Luke 16:19-31.

"What comes out of a person is what defiles him. For from within, out of the heart of man, come evil thoughts, sexual immorality[207] theft, murder, adultery, coveting, wickedness, deceit, sensuality, envy, slander, pride, foolishness. All of these evil things come from within, and they defile a person."[208]

Similarly, Jesus' "Sermon on the Mount" seems to include a condemnation of those who only keep the commandments outwardly, but not from the heart. [209] For example, those who might think they've kept the commandment "thou shall not murder" even though they harbor hatred and forgiveness in their heart. Or those who think they are holy because they have never physically committed adultery—but harbor lust in their hearts.

Jesus warned that "Everyone who sins is a slave to sin."[210] When Jesus spoke to the woman at the well, he confronted her about her sin, i.e. that she was living with someone who was not her husband![211] After Jesus healed a disabled man Jesus later found him and warned him to "Stop sinning or something worse may happen to you."[212] Jesus was certainly not teaching that disability is the result of sin (see John 9:1-3), but in this particular case Jesus was warning this man that flaunting the grace of God shown to him may have serious consequences.

John 7:53-8:11 is about the grace of Jesus in excusing the woman caught in adultery. In this disputed passage[213] the "teachers of the law and the Pharisees brought to Jesus

---

207   In a Jewish culture this prohibition would have included all those sexual sins in Leviticus 18 and 20: e.g. adultery, sex with close relatives, sex with people of the same sex and sex with animals.
208   Mark 7:20-23//Matthew 15:17-20.
209   Matthew 7:21-48.
210   John 8:34. This is exactly what Paul taught as well, see Romans 6:16.
211   John 4:18.
212   John 5:14.
213   The earliest manuscripts of the John do not contain this passage. Some argue—plausibly in my view—that this was a true story that John had taught and was added by John's disciples when they copied his Gospel.

a woman caught in adultery." Jesus said, "Let any one of you who is without sin the first to throw a stone at her." After the accusers had left, Jesus asked the woman, "Has no one condemned you?" She said, "No one, sir." Jesus responded, "Then neither do I condemn you" but then he added, "Go now and *leave your life of sin*."[214] The point is that Jesus' grace did not just excuse her to continue living in sin.

After discussing adultery in Matthew 5:27-30, Jesus said that someone who even looks at a woman lustfully "has already committed adultery with her in his heart." This would certainly have implications for the viewing of pornography! Jesus then warned that sin must be dealt with drastically. He said, "If your right eye causes you to sin, gouge it out and throw it away" or if your "right hand causes you to sin, cut it off and throw it away." Jesus was certainly not teaching that you should literally maim yourself! He was using hyperbole to make memorable the important point that sin is very serious in the eyes of God and we should take drastic measures to avoid it. Why? Jesus said, "It is better for you to lose one part of your body than for your whole body to go into hell"![215] So important was this principle that it was repeated again in Matthew 18:8-9, this time adding that if your foot causes you to sin, cut it off.[216]

In Matthew 13:41-43 Jesus warned that at the final judgment he will send out his angel to "weed out of his kingdom everything that causes sin and all who do evil. They will throw them into the fiery furnace, where there will be weeping and gnashing of teeth." Unlike so much of contemporary "Christianity," Jesus apparently took sin very seriously and called people to repentance.

True repentance is not just being sorry for particular

---

214   Emphasis mine.
215   Matthew 5:27-30.
216   See also Mark 9:43-47

sins. Even Judas felt sorrowful for betraying Jesus. Repentance begins with a recognition that we are not our own. We belong to our Creator, the King. We need to repent of our autonomy or independence from the King. We need to repent of our idolatry, that is, of putting other things before our king. This, of course, also involves repentance of our acts of rebellion or sin against the King's commands. Repentance, *metanoia* (μετανοια) in Greek, literally means to have a change of mind, or as we might say, a change of heart. It is seeing sin as the horrible rebellion against our King that it is, coupled with a genuine desire to turn.

So why did Paul usually call people to faith when Jesus called them to repentance? The answer is that Jesus also people to faith[217] just as Paul called also called people to repentance.[218] Repentance and faith are like two sides of the same coin. Repentance involves a heart turning *away* from sin whereas faith is the heart turning *toward* the Lord. Repentance alone is not enough. We must not only turn *from* our sin, we must turn *to* our King as the only hope of being saved from the penalty of sin. So instead of putting ourselves first, or putting anyone or anything first, people are to turn to the King and give him their highest allegiance. In other words, they are to turn to him in faith.

The Gospel of Luke gives a good illustration of what such faith looks like.[219] Luke recorded the story of how Jesus was sharing a meal with a group of religious leaders when suddenly a woman came in. She was crying. Since she was described as a sinner in the passage—four times![220]—and since no other reason for the tears were given, and since the ultimate result of the story was forgiveness of her sins, we are

---

217   E.g. John 6:29-64; 8:24; John 9:35-38; 10:25-26; 13:19; 14:10, 11, 29; 16:9.
218   Romans 2:4; 2 Corinthians 7:10; 2 Timothy 2:25.
219   Luke 7:36-50.
220   Luke 7:37; 39; 47, 48.

led to believe that she was sorrowfully repentant for her sin.

The religious leaders at this dinner were described as "reclining at table," which meant that they were lying down on their left side, propping their head up with their left hand while eating with their right hand. Their feet would have been extended out away from the very short "table" containing the food. The woman bypassed the religious leaders and went straight to Jesus. She would have had to have gotten down on her knees as she kissed Jesus' feet, anointed them with oil and wiped them off with her hair.

A Pharisee named Simon was indignant. If Jesus were a prophet, surely he would know what kind of woman this was and would not let her touch him. Jesus pointed out to Simon that when Jesus had come in to Simon's house, Simon had not even extended the basic courtesies of hospitality to Jesus, whereas this woman had wet Jesus' feet with her tears and wiped them with her hair and anointed them with ointment. Jesus said, "Therefore I tell you, her sins, which are many, are forgiven—for she loved much." Then he told the woman that her sins were forgiven and that *her faith* has saved her.[221]

But wait! What faith? Nothing in this passage said anything about faith.

We are apparently being led to believe that this woman's sorrow (repentance) over her sin and her loving devotion to Jesus is the very definition of saving faith! Contrary to popular belief, saving faith is not "just believing what God says he will do" as the popular children's song says.[222] The book of James says that even the demons believe that—and

---

221   Luke 7:36-50.
222   http://cefpress.com/Faith-Is-Just-Believing.html. Child Evangelism Fellowship has a song that says, "Faith is just believing what God says he will do. He will never fail us, his promises are true. If we but believe him, his children we become. Faith is just believing, this wondrous thing is done." Child Evangelism Fellowship is a wonderful organization, but their song is not biblical.

shudder![223] Neither is saving faith just about believing certain facts about Jesus, as important as those facts certainly are (e.g. his deity and resurrection). Even the demons believe facts about Jesus.

Some will say that saving faith is about trusting Jesus to take away your sins. They use the example of a chair. It is not enough just to believe the chair exists—you must also trust it enough to sit in it. Likewise, saving faith is about trusting Jesus to take away your sins and bring us to heaven. But according to the Gospel of Matthew, there are wicked people who apparently trust that Jesus will take them to heaven—but Jesus will one day tell them "Depart from me, I never knew you."[224] Saving faith is not just about trusting that Jesus will take you to heaven.

Nor does salvation come merely by saying a prayer to "ask Jesus into your heart."[225] This idea comes from Revelation 3:20 in which Jesus says, "Here I am! I stand at the door and knock. If anyone hears my voice and opens the door, I will come in and eat with him, and he with me." We assume that Jesus is speaking of the door to our heart" and that all we have to do is say a prayer to ask him in. But the context is not about saying a prayer. The context deals with repentance and "overcoming."[226]

It's not that there is anything wrong with "asking Jesus into your heart" or "making a decision for Christ," or "accepting Christ" as long as people understand that these are not magical formulas to keep us out of hell, but are just "short-hand" phrases we use to refer to genuine repentance and faith.

---

223   James 2:19.
224   Mt 7:22-23.
225   Revelation 3:20
226   Revelation 3:19-21.

Saving faith is about sincerely repenting of our sin and rebellion against the King, and turning our hearts over to him in loving devotion, swearing allegiance, so to speak, to our King above all else!

Chapter Nine

Obedience to the King
That Comes from Faith

So saving faith is not just about those who call Jesus "Lord, Lord," but about those who, out of a heart of loving devotion to our King, *follow him and obey him.*[227] After all, it was Jesus who said, "If you love me *you will keep my commandments.*"[228] He said that anyone who loves him *"will keep my word."*[229] Jesus said it is those who do not keep his commandments who do not love him.[230] In fact, according to John, "Whoever says I know him but does not keep his commandments is a liar..."! [231] In response to a woman who blessed him, Jesus said, "Blessed rather are those who hear the Word of God *and obey it.*"[232] In fact, Jesus said that it was those *who keep his Word* who shall not see death.[233] On the other hand, Jesus taught, "the one who hears my words and does not put them into practice"—in other words, the one who hears his word and does not obey—"is like a man who built a house on the ground without a foundation. The moment the torrent struck that house it collapsed and its destruction was complete."[234]

After warning that "The man who loves his life will lose

227   Matthew 7:21-23; Romans 2:6-8; Galatians 5:18-21; Ephesians 5:3-6; 1 Cor. 6:9-10; James 2:14-26; Hebrews 11; Rev 22:15.
228   John 14:15. The Greek could be imperative rather than indicative: "If you love me, keep my commandments."
229   John 14:23-24, cf. John 15:10.
230   John 14:24.
231   1 John.2:4.
232   Luke 11:28.
233   John 8:51-52, cf. John8:31.
234   Luke 6:49.

it, while the man who hates his life in this world will keep it for eternal life," Jesus added, "Whoever serves me must follow me."[235] Following Jesus was never just a matter of traveling all over Galilee with Jesus. Jesus apparently never demanded that Mary, Martha and Lazarus sell their home and follow him around on his preaching trips. In fact, the man from whom Jesus cast out demons into a herd of swine even begged to follow Jesus. Jesus told him to go back home and tell what great things God had done for him. Neither is following Jesus about growing long hair and a beard and keeping Jewish dietary laws and feast days! Following Jesus is about obeying what he taught.

Evangelicals rightly place a great deal of emphasis on Jesus' command to go into all the world to make disciples but we don't often hear as much about that fact that making disciples involves "teaching them *to obey* everything I have commanded you."[236] We are not really making disciples unless we are teaching people to obey our King and we are not even following him ourselves if we are not striving to follow his teachings in our own life.

What Jesus taught elsewhere about grace[237] shows, however, that he was not thinking of salvation by works but rather, as Paul would later write, an "obedience that comes from faith."[238] Throughout history some people have believed

---

235   John 12:25-26.
236   Matthew 28:19-20.
237   For example, the stories of Jesus eating in the Pharisee's home (Luke 7), the Prodigal Son (Luke15:11-32), the Pharisee and sinner in the Temple (Luke 18), and the landowner who hired people in the marketplace (Matthew 21:1-16), are all stories of God's grace.
238   Romans 1:5; 16:26. The phrase is "υπακοην πιστεως" which literally means "obedience of faith." This could be translated "obedience that *is* faith" or "obedience that *comes from* faith." While both are true, the latter best fits the context of Romans in which Paul writes, "It is not the hearers of the law who are righteous before God, but the *doers of the law* who will be justified (Romans 2:13, cf. Romans 2:8) and that "you who were once slaves of sin have become obedient from the heart" (Romans 6:17). Those who believe the phrase should be translated "obedience that is faith" might appeal to Jesus' words in John 6:29: "This is the work of God that you believe in him whom he has sent." In the context of John 6,

that Paul's teaching on salvation by grace apart from works contradicted the teachings of Jesus' teaching on obedience, but this is not true.

Many people might be surprised to learn how much emphasis Paul actually places on obedience. For example, Paul writes, "It is not the hearers of the law who are righteous before God, but the *doers of the law* who will be justified.[239] Roughly half of Paul's letter to the Ephesians explains how we should live in obedience to God. Virtually the entire book of First Corinthians tells how Christians should live the Christian life; and in what may be regarded as the purpose statement for First Timothy, Paul writes, "I am writing these things to you so that...you may know how one *ought to behave* in the household of God."[240]

Paul writes that those who "are self-seeking and *do not obey* the truth" are destined for wrath and fury[241] and that God will one day inflict vengeance in flaming fire on those who "do not *obey* the gospel...."[242] Paul went so far as to warn his readers that those who practiced sexual immorality, homosexuality, adultery, idolatry, drunkenness, theft, greed et al. would not inherit the kingdom of God.[243] In fact, to his critics who said we should just live in sin to show how gracious God really is, Paul responded, "Their condemnation is just!"[244]

This emphasis on obedience appears throughout the entire New Testament. John, for example, wrote "...whoever does not *obey* the Son shall not see life, but the wrath of God

---

however, Jesus said that eternal life involved "eating his flesh and drinking his blood," which metaphorically speaks of a deep love, devotion and union with Christ which can only result in obedience.

239   Romans 2:13.
240   1 Tim.3:14-15.
241   Romans 2:8.
242   2 Thessalonians 1:8.
243   1 Corinthians 6:9-11; cf. Galatians 5:16-25.
244   Romans 3:8; cf. 6:1.

remains on him."[245] The Book of Acts says God has given his Holy Spirit "to those who *obey* him."[246] The writer of Hebrews said that Jesus is "the source of eternal salvation to all who *obey* him."[247] Peter writes to "...*make every effort* to add to your faith goodness...knowledge...self-control...perseverance... godliness...brotherly kindness; and...love."[248] And both Peter and Jude absolutely come unglued against "ungodly people, who pervert the grace of our God into sensuality."[249]

Obedience, however, is not a popular topic in modern Christianity. In fact, anyone who would dare to preach obedience too strongly is bound to be attacked as self-righteous, judgmental, and legalistic![250] The critic will insist that Christians are free from the law and that Christianity is not about rules and regulations but about relationship, compassion and community. The critic may point out, for example, that Jesus said, "It is the Spirit who gives life; the flesh is no help at all."[251] That's true, but in that passage, Jesus immediately follows up with, "*The words* that I have spoken to you are *spirit and life*,"[252] which means that "Jesus' words are life-giving because they are infused by the Spirit, who rests on Jesus to an unlimited degree.[253] In other words, just because "It is the Spirit who gives life" this does not negate the importance of living in obedience to the life-giving,

---

245   John 3:36.
246   Acts 5:32.
247   Hebrews 5:9.
248   Second Peter 1:5-7, emphasis mine.
249   Jude 4, cf. 2 Peter 2.
250   Although many Christians have certainly been self-righteous and hypocritical, it doesn't take much discernment to realize that merely teaching what the Bible says does not automatically make someone a self-righteous, judgmental or legalistic. Samuel Stoesz writes, "The result of secular influence is that immorality is tolerated even in so-called evangelical circles" (Stoesz, Samuel. *Sanctification; an Alliance distinctive*. [Camp Hill, PA : Christian Publications, 1992], 6).
251   John 6:63.
252   John 6:63.
253   John 1:33; 3:34. Cf. Kostenberger, Andreas J. *A Theology of John's Gospel and Letters*. (Grand Rapids : Zondervan, 2009), 394.

Spirit-infused words of Jesus.

But doesn't Paul say, "Where the Spirit of the Lord is, there is freedom."[254] Doesn't Paul insist that "we are released from the law...so that we serve in the new way of the Spirit."[255] Doesn't he also say, "The letter kills, but the Spirit gives life."[256] Isn't Paul arguing that we are now free from the law and legalism?

Absolutely! But Paul was refuting the false notion that keeping rules, regulations or rituals can make us right before God. In Christ we are free from such legalism, but Paul never taught that we are free to live in sin. For example, in Romans Paul taught that, "the law of the Spirit of life has set you free in Christ Jesus from the law of sin and death," but in the same letter Paul wrote that those who are *in the Spirit* "put to death" the evil behaviors of the body.[257]

Galatians is another letter in which Paul argued so fervently for our freedom from the law, writing that we "were called to freedom," but in practically the same breath he went on to exhort, "*walk by the Spirit*, and you will not gratify the desires of the flesh." Paul tied the work of the Spirit to obedience saying "if we live by the Spirit, let us also walk by the Spirit."[258]

Paul then closed his letter to the Galatians with extended exhortations to godly behavior and serious warnings against sin.[259] For example, Paul wrote that if you are truly *led by the Spirit* you will exhibit the fruit of the Spirit; love, joy, peace, kindness, goodness, etc., rather than the works of the flesh which are "sexual immorality, impurity, sensuality, idolatry, sorcery, enmity, strife, jealousy, fits of anger, rivalries,

---

254   2 Corinthians 3:17.
255   Romans 7:6.
256   2 Corinthians 3:6.
257   Romans 8:13.
258   Galatians 5:13-26.
259   Galatians 5:16-6:10.

dissensions, divisions, envy, drunkenness, orgies" etc. Paul wrote that those who practice such things "will not inherit the Kingdom of God."[260]

The freedom of which Paul wrote is freedom from thinking we have to work or strive to be good enough to merit God's forgiveness and justification, but for Paul, being called to "freedom" never meant freedom to sin and never eliminates the need to walk by the Spirit in obedience to God.

It cannot be emphasized too strongly that this teaching on obedience is not salvation by works. Both Jesus and Paul taught that we are saved by grace.[261] For example, in Jesus' parable of the Pharisee and the tax collector, the Pharisee prayed, "God thank you that I am not like other men—robbers, evildoers, adulterers—or even like this tax collector. I fast twice a week and give a tenth of all I get." The tax collector, on the other hand did not appeal to any good works but threw himself on God's grace, beating his chest and pleading, "God have mercy on me, a sinner." Jesus said it was the tax collector that was made right with God, not the Pharisee. In other words, the man who humbly threw himself on God's mercy and grace was justified, not the man who self-righteously thought he was good enough to earn God's favor.

Paul strongly emphasized this theme of grace. In his letter to the Galatians, Paul wrote, "know that a man is not justified by observing the law, but by faith in Jesus Christ. So too, we have put or faith in Christ Jesus that we may be justified by faith in Christ and not by observing the law, because by observing the law no one will be justified."[262] In

---

260   Galatians 5:13-26. Paul is not saying that people who fall into such sins through weakness of the flesh are not saved. Even Paul acknowledges that Christians can at times be fleshly or "carnal" (1 Corinthians 3:1-3, cf. Romans 7:14-22 which many scholars believe to be autobiographical). Paul is saying that those who willfully and unrepentantly engage in lifestyles characterized by this kind of sin are not really saved at all.

261   Luke 18:9-14; Romans 3:24; 4:16; 5:15, 17; 11:6; Galatians 2:21; Ephesians 2:5, 8-10; Titus 3:5.

262   Galatians 2:16.

Romans Paul wrote that "no one will be declared righteous in his [God's] sight by observing the law…"[263] but that we are "justified freely by his grace through the redemption that is came by Christ Jesus."[264] This righteousness and redemption come "through faith in Jesus Christ to all who believe."[265] Paul wrote that we are "justified by faith apart from observing the law." [266]

In his letter to the Ephesians Paul wrote, For it is by grace you have been saved through faith—and this not from yourselves, it is the gift of God—not by works, so that no one can boast." Paul goes on to add, however, that "we are his workmanship, created in Christ Jesus to do good works…."[267]

In Second Timothy Paul wrote of God "who has saved us and called us to a holy life—not because of anything we have done but because of his own purpose and grace."[268] Similarly, Paul wrote to Titus saying that "God our Savior… saved us, not because of righteous things we had done, but because of his mercy."[269]

So while Paul strongly emphasized that salvation comes only by God's grace through faith, never on the basis of good things we have done, Paul just as strongly emphases the fact that "we are his workmanship in Christ Jesus created for good works.[270] Just as a wood fire in the fireplace produces smoke in the chimney, so faith produces works. Good works cannot help but come from a heart that is genuinely and lovingly devoted to our King. Paul would call such good works the "obedience that comes from faith."[271] But such works do nothing to save

---

263   Romans 3:20.
264   Romans 3:24.
265   Romans 3:22.
266   Romans 3:28.
267   Ephesians 2:8-10.
268   Second Timothy 1:9.
269   Titus 3:5.
270   Ephesians 2:8-10.
271   Romans 1:5; 16:26.

us. Just as smoke is the byproduct of a wood fire, works are the byproduct of faith, a deep loving devotion to Christ working through the power of the Holy Spirit.

Jesus once said, "I seek not to please myself but him who sent me."[272] So also we should seek to please our King. The process of living a life which is more and more obedient, more pleasing to our King is called, "sanctification." Unfortunately, there are no magic formulas for sanctification. Sanctification or holiness is sometimes just hard work. For example, Paul wrote: "*Do not let* sin reign in your mortal body,"[273] "*Do not offer* the parts of your body to sin,"[274] "*Cast off* the works of darkness and *put on* the armor of light."[275] Paul wrote that just as we once made our bodies available to impurity and wickedness, we must now make them "slaves to righteousness leading to sanctification."[276] There is really nothing mystical or mysterious about all this. Paul says just do it, or don't do it as the case may be. We don't even have to contemplate it, pray about it or meditate on it! Just obey it!

Of course this is all very easy to write but often so very hard to obey. In fact, it is nearly impossible to preach or teach on biblical obedience without being painfully aware of how far we personally fall short. While sanctification can be a crisis experience, it is also a long progressive journey. On this journey, temptation can often seem overwhelming. We need to be constantly aware that "we do not wrestle against flesh and blood, but against...the spiritual forces of evil."[277] We need to understand that our "adversary the Devil prowls around like a roaring lion seeking someone to devour."[278]

272   John 5:30 in the NIV. Literally: "I do not seek my will but the will of him who sent me."
273   Romans 6:12.
274   Romans 6:13.
275   Romans 13:12.
276   Romans 6:19.
277   Ephesians 6:12.
278   1 Peter 5:8.

Paul counseled that we should put on the "armor of God" including the "Sword of the Spirit which is the Word of God."[279] If we are not aware of what the Word of God teaches, we will not know how to please God in any given situation. We may also need to be on the lookout for that "way of escape" Paul talks about[280] in order to avoid overwhelming temptation. For example, one way to avoid temptation is often to choose not to go to places where we know temptation will be strong.

Sometimes we may need to seek someone who will keep us accountable.[281] In more severe cases like obsessive-compulsive disorders involving sin, Christian counseling or psychiatry may be helpful. In any case, we *always* need to pray for the Spirit's wisdom and power, and we certainly need to sincerely repent when we sin—and we *will* sin. John writes that "if we say we have no sin we deceive ourselves and the truth is not in us."[282] The biblical hall of fame is populated with repentant sinners: Moses the murderer, Samson the playboy, David the adulterer, Jonah the rebel, Peter the denier of Jesus, Paul the persecutor of Christians, etc. Being saved does not mean we never sin but it does mean that when we fall, we sincerely repent and, by the power of the Holy Spirit, strive once again to live a life of obedience which is pleasing to our King.

Some will protest, however, that we should stop striving to please God since we are already accepted and pleasing in his sight. There is some truth to this. Positional sanctification is the biblical teaching expressed in Second Corinthians 5:21 that "God made him who had no sin [Jesus] to be sin for us, so that in him we might become

---

279   Ephesians 6:17.
280   1 Corinthians 10:13.
281   James 5:16.
282   1 John 1:8.

the righteousness of God." In other words, positional sanctification is the idea that Jesus took our sin to the cross, and we are clothed with his righteousness. Even though we still sin, God sees believers through the lens, so to speak, of Christ's righteousness.

This however, does not change the fact that obedience to Jesus our King *is* pleasing to God. For example, my children are my children and I love them more than life itself. There is nothing they could do to earn the right to become my children and there is nothing they could do to earn my love—they already have it. But when they were growing up there were certainly good behaviors that were pleasing to dad and bad behaviors that were not pleasing to dad, bad behaviors which often resulted in discipline.[283]

The fact that we should strive to please God is a repeated theme in the New Testament. Jesus, speaking of the Father, said, "I always do what pleases him."[284] Paul, following the example of Jesus, says that he speaks "not to please man, but *to please God.*"[285] He urges the Colossians to live their lives "in a manner worthy of the Lord, *fully pleasing to him.*"[286] Similarly, Paul tells the Philippians to conduct themselves "in a manner worthy of the gospel of Christ."[287] Paul reminds the Thessalonians that he taught them how they "ought to walk and *to please God.*"[288] He tells the Philippians that their sacrificial gift was *"pleasing to God."*[289] He tells Timothy that living a peaceful, quiet, godly life *"is pleasing* in the sight of God our Savior."[290] By contrast, Paul writes that "those who

---

283   Hebrews 12:5-6.
284   John 8:29.
285   1 Thessalonians 2:4.
286   Colossians 1:10.
287   Philippians 1:27.
288   1 Thessalonians 4:1.
289   Philippians 4:18.
290   1 Timothy 2:3, cf. 1 Timothy 5:3-4.

are in the flesh cannot please God."[291] Similarly the author of
Hebrews exhorts, "Do not neglect to do good and to share
what you have, for such sacrifices *are pleasing to God*."[292] The
writer of Hebrews—reminding us that pleasing God is not a
matter of human effort alone, but of divine empowerment—
closes his book with a benediction: "May the God of peace...
equip you with everything good for doing his will, and may
he work in us *what is pleasing to him*...."[293] The idea that we
should strive to please God in our daily lives is not just an
isolated New Testament teaching.

If we are truly, lovingly devoted to our Lord, the King,
we will *want* to live a life pleasing to him and will sincerely
repent when we fail. In fact, those who really *do not want*
to live a life pleasing to the King and do not sincerely repent
when they sin, need to follow Paul's exhortation to examine
themselves to see whether they are really saved at all.[294]

None of us follow King Jesus perfectly, of course[295] but
the fundamental disposition or direction of our heart is either
"allegiance" to Jesus our King, or allegiance to some idol,
whether that idol is some religion, or our money, our things,
or even ourselves. This is what Paul is writing about in Romans
8:5-8.

> Those who are dominated by the sinful nature
> think about sinful things, but those who are
> controlled by the Holy Spirit think about things
> that please the Spirit. So letting your sinful nature
> control your mind leads to death. But letting the
> Spirit control your mind leads to life and peace.
> For the sinful nature is always hostile to God. It
> never did obey God's laws, and it never will. That's
> why those who are still under the control of their
> sinful nature can never please God.[296]

291	Romans 8:8.
292	Hebrews 13:16.
293	Hebrews 13:20a, 21.
294	2 Corinthians 3:15.
295	1 John 1:8-10.
296	Romans 8:5-8. NLT

There is a bottom-line sense in which the fundamental disposition or direction of people's hearts is to have a mind, as Paul calls it, either "dominated by the sinful nature" or "controlled by the Holy Spirit." There are no other possibilities. Those who "set their minds on the things of the Spirit" (ESV), have life and peace. According to Paul, those who "set their minds on things of the flesh (ESV)—i.e. those for whom the "flesh" and this life are more important to them than God, are "hostile to God" and "cannot please God."

As the Protestant scholar, William Hendriksen puts it,

> Those who live according to the flesh allow their lives to be basically determined by their sinful human nature. They set their minds on—are most deeply interested in, constantly talk about, engage and glory in—the things pertaining to the flesh, that is, to sinful human nature. Those who live according to the Spirit, and therefore submit to the Spirit's direction, concentrate their attention on, and specialize in, whatever is dear to the Spirit... Paul is reminding the members of the church in Rome that it is impossible to be on both sides at once; that is, the *basic*—this adjective should be stressed!—disposition or direction of our lives is either on God's side or on the side of sinful human nature. If a person persists in being worldly, he is on the side of the world and must expect the world's doom.[297]

The Roman Catholic scholar, Frank Matera, says it more concisely, "...the Spirit of God is presently at work in the lives of the justified so that they can live in a way pleasing to God (8:4-10)."[298]

Those whose minds are set on "things of the flesh" are those whose whole life centers on things like power, status, keeping up with the Joneses, the next raise, the next promotion, the next party, a bigger house, a new car (or

---

297   William Hendriksen. *Romans* (*New Testament Commentary Series*), (Grand Rapids: Baker, 1981), 248-249.
298   Frank J. Matera. *God's Saving Grace; A Pauline Theology*. (Grand Rapids : Eerdmans, 2012), 237.

motorcycle, boat, jet ski, etc.).[299] It's not that such things are necessarily wrong in themselves, but if these are the primary focus of our life rather than the "things of the Spirit" or the love of our King, Paul says that we can expect (spiritual) death.[300]

Genuine saving faith involves a heart that sincerely wants to avoid those things which are displeasing to our King and to practice those things that we know will please him.[301] There are people who claim to be Christians, however, who have no real love for the Lord and no real desire to serve him, and yet think they are saved merely because they have "accepted Christ" or said a prayer to "ask Jesus into their hearts," [302] or who trust that he will take them to heaven. They have been seriously misled or are deceiving themselves. As John Calvin wrote, "all Scripture cries out" against such a notion.[303]

As mentioned earlier, it's not that there is anything wrong with "making a decision for Christ," or "accepting Christ" or "asking Jesus into your heart" as long as you understand that these are just short-hand phrases we use to refer to a heart of repentance and loving devotion to Jesus the King, and are not some magical formulas you recite to give you "fire insurance" and keep you out of hell.

---

299   John would call these things "the desires of the flesh and the desires of the eyes and the pride in possessions" and says that the love of the Father is not in those whose life centers on these things (First John 1:15-16).

300   Romans 8:6-8.

301   2 Corinthians 5:9; 1 Thessalonians 2:4; 4:1; Ephesians 5:10; Philippians 4:18; Colossians 1:10; 1 Timothy 5:4; Hebrews 11:6; 13:16; 21; Romans 8:8.

302   Revelation 1:20 cannot be divorced from the immediate context in Revelation 1:15-16; 2:20-23; cf. 22:13-19. The so-called "sinner's prayer in which someone "asks Jesus into their heart" is often the initial expression of genuine faith but no one should assume that mechanically saying this prayer (apart from repentance/faith) saves anyone.

303   John Calvin wrote about people who "are touched with no fear of God, no sense of piety, nevertheless believe whatever it is necessary to know for salvation...And they dignify that persuasion, devoid of the fear of God, with the name 'faith' even though all Scripture cries out against it" (John Calvin. *Institutes of the Christian Religion*. III.2. 8).

Chapter Ten

But that's just *your* interpretation!

This idea that genuine faith involves a change of heart which results in a change in lifestyle is not just my interpretation or some new heresy. It is orthodox Christian doctrine. As far back as AD 95 Clement of Rome wrote, "Let us not merely call Him Lord, for that will not save us. For He says, 'Not everyone who says to me Lord, Lord, will be saved, but him who does what is right."[304]

Similarly, Martin Luther (1483-1546) wrote:

> When we have thus taught faith In Christ, then do we teach also good works. Because thou hast laid hold upon Christ by faith, through whom thou art made righteous, begin now to work well. Love God and thy neighbor, call upon God, give thanks unto him, praise him, confess him. Do good to thy neighbor and serve him...*These are good works indeed, which flow out of this faith.*[305]

Luther also wrote,

> ....it is impossible, indeed to separate works from faith, just as it is impossible to separate heat and light from fire.[306]

One of the leading reformers associated with Luther was Philip Melanchthon (1497-1560) who wrote, "*The Holy Spirit is not in a heart in which there is no fear of God*, but instead a continuous defiance."[307] In other words, a heart

---

304   Cyril C. Richardson, ed. *Early Christian Fathers* (New York : Macmillan, 1970), 177; quoted from John MacArthur. *The Gospel According to Jesus*. Rev. ed. (Grand Rapids : Zondervan, 1994), 256.

305   John Dillenberger, ed., Martin Luther (New York : Doubleday, 1961), 111-112; quoted from John MacArthur. *The Gospel According to Jesus*. Rev. ed. (Grand Rapids : Zondervan), 258. Emphasis mine.

306   Dillenberger, 23-24; MacArthur, 259.

307   Clyde L. Manschreck, ed. And trans., *Melancthon on Christian Doctrine* (Grand

characterized by a fundamental defiance against God is not a heart indwelt by the Holy Spirit, and as Paul said, "if anyone does not have the Spirit of Christ, he does not belong to Christ.[308]

About the same time as Luther, the reformer, John Calvin (1509-1564) wrote about people who:

> are touched with no fear of God, no sense of piety, nevertheless believe whatever it is neces- sary to know for salvation...And they dignify that persuasion, devoid of the fear of God, with the name 'faith' even though all Scripture cries out against it." "They would have faith to be an assent by which any despiser of God may receive what is offered from Scripture." Faith, Calvin writes, "is more of the heart than of the brain, and more of the disposition than of the understanding." "It fol- lows that faith can in no wise be separated from a devout disposition.[309]

The Puritan, Thomas Vincent (1634-1678) explained the Westminster Shorter Catechism (1674) saying:

> Repentance unto life is a saving grace, whereby a sinner, out of a true sense of his sin, and ap- prehension of the mercy of God in Christ, doth with grief and hatred of his sin, turn from it unto God, with full purpose of, and endeavor after, new obedience.[310]

In 1693 another Puritan, Thomas Manton (1620-1677) wrote, "Works are an evidence of true faith."[311] In the 1700's the popular Bible commentator and preacher, Matthew Henry wrote,

---

Rapids : Baker, 1965), 182; quoted from John MacArthur. *The Gospel According to Jesus*. Rev. ed. Grand Rapids : Zondervan,259. Emphasis mine.

308   Romans 8:9.

309   John Calvin. *Institutes of the Christian Religion*. Philadelphia : Westminster Press, 1960. III.2. 8.

310   Thomas Vincent, *The Shorter Catechism of the Westminster Assembly Explained and Proved from Scripture* (Edinburgh : Banner of Truth, 1980), 226-231; quoted from John MacArthur. *The Gospel According to Jesus*. Rev. ed. (Grand Rapids : Zondervan), 262.

311   Thomas Manton, *A Commentary on James* (Edinburgh : Banner of Truth, 1963), 239; quoted from John MacArthur. *The Gospel According to Jesus*. Rev. ed. (Grand Rapids : Zondervan), 264.

We are too apt to rest in a bare profession of faith, and to think that this will save us; it is a cheap and easy religion to say, 'We believe the articles of the Christian faith;' but it is a great delusion to imagine that this is enough to bring us to heaven."[312]

In the late seventeenth and early eighteenth centuries, a Scottish church leader named Thomas Boston (1676-1732) wrote, "We are to receive Christ as our King, renouncing the domination of sin, death, the devil, and the world, and wholly giving up ourselves to him to be ruled by him as our head."[313]

George Whitefield (1714-1770), the great British preacher and revivalist who helped spread the Great Awakening in America, wrote,

...for though...good works, which are the fruits of faith, cannot put away our sins, or endure the severity of God's judgment (that is, cannot justify us), yet they follow after justification, and do spring out necessarily of a true and lively faith."[314]

In 1767 a prominent British Baptist minister named James Gill wrote,

In subjection to him, as King of saints; they not only receive him as their Prophet, to teach and instruct them...; and as their Priest, by whose sacrifice their sins are expiated; but *as their King to whose law and ordinances they cheerfully submit...* from a principle of love to him, keep and observe them."[315]

Charles Haddon Spurgeon (1834-1892) was one of the

312　　Matthew Henry, *Commentary on the Whole Bible* (Old Tappan, N.J. : Revell, n.d.), 981-983; quoted from John MacArthur. *The Gospel According to Jesus*. Rev. ed. (Grand Rapids : Zondervan), 264.

313　　Thomas Boston, "A Brief Explication of the First Part of the Assembly's Shorter Catechism," in *The Complete Works of the Late Rev. Thomas Boston, Ettrick*, 12 vols. (Wheaton, Ill." Roberts, 1980 reprint), 7:67-68; quoted from John MacArthur. *The Gospel According to Jesus*. Rev. ed. (Grand Rapids : Zondervan), 265.

314　　George Whitefield, *Journals* (Edinburgh P: Banner of Truth, 1960), 323-24; quoted from John MacArthur. *The Gospel According to Jesus*. Rev. ed. (Grand Rapids : Zondervan), 265.

315　　John Gill, *A Body of Divinity* (Grand Rapids : Sovereign Grace, 1971), 552; quoted from John MacArthur. *The Gospel According to Jesus*. Rev. ed. (Grand Rapids : Zondervan), 267. Emphasis mine.

most prominent preachers of his time. Spurgeon wrote,

> Another proof of the conquest of a soul for Christ
> will be found in a real change of life. If the man
> does not live differently from what he did be-
> fore, both at home and abroad, his repentances
> needs to be repented of, and his conversion is a
> fiction."[316]

Spurgeon also wrote,

> *If a man is not desiring to live a holy life* in the
> sight of God, with the help of the Holy Spirit, he
> is still 'in the gall of bitterness, and in the bond
> of iniquity.'...The idea of 'saving faith' apart from
> good works, is ridiculous. The saved man is not a
> perfect man, but his heart's desire is to become
> perfect."[317]

R.A. Torrey (1856-1928), associated with the Christian
and Missionary Alliance and one time president of Moody
Bible Institute wrote the following in a textbook on personal
evangelism: "Lead him as directly as you can to accept Jesus
Christ as a personal Saviour, and to surrender to Him as his
Lord and Master."[318]

W.H. Griffith Thomas (1861-1924), the dispensationalist
founder of Dallas Theological Seminary wrote,

> We have to acknowledge Christ as our Lord. Sin
> is rebellion, and it is only as we surrender to him
> as Lord that we receive our pardon from Him
> as our Savior. We have to admit Him to reign on
> the throne of the heart, and it is only when He is
> glorified in our hearts as King that the Holy Spirit
> enters and abides.[319]

---

316   Charles H. Spurgeon, *The Soul Winner* (Passadena, Tex. : Pilgrim, 1978), 32-
33; quoted from John MacArthur. *The Gospel According to Jesus*. Rev. ed. (Grand Rapids :
Zondervan), 267.
317   Charles H. Spurgeon, *The Soul Winner* (Passadena, Tex. : Pilgrim), 1978, 32-
33; quoted from John MacArthur. *The Gospel According to Jesus*. Rev. ed. (Grand Rapids :
Zondervan), 268. Emphasis mine.
318   R.A. Torrey. *How to work for Christ* (Old Tappan, NJ. : Revell, n.d.), 32; quoted from
John MacArthur. *The Gospel According to Jesus*. Rev. ed. (Grand Rapids : Zondervan), 269.
319   W.H. Griffith Thomas, *St. Paul's Epistle to the Romans* (Grand Rapids : Eerdmans,
n.d.), 371; quoted from John MacArthur. *The Gospel According to Jesus*. Rev. ed. (Grand Rapids
: Zondervan),269-270.

The prominent Christian evangelist and biblical scholar, A.W. Pink (1886-1952) wrote,

> Those preachers who tell sinners they may be saved without forsaking their idols, without repenting, without surrendering to the Lordship of Christ, are as erroneous and dangerous as others who insist that salvation is by works and that heaven must be earned by our own efforts.[320]

A.W. Tozer (1897-1963), a C&MA pastor and author of over 40 books wrote,

> [Years ago] no one would ever dare to rise in a meeting and say, 'I am a Christian' if he had not surrendered his whole being to God and had taken Jesus Christ as his Lord as well as his Saviour, and had brought himself under obedience to the will of the Lord.[321]

Finally, lest anyone think that the definition of repentance and faith presented in this book is just a Protestant teaching, it is worth noting that even the Roman Catholic Church agrees. The Catholic Church defines repentance as:

> ...a radical reorientation of our whole life, a conversion to God with all our heart...a turning away from evil with a repugnance toward the evil actions we have committed. At the same time it entails the desire and resolution to change one's life, with hope in God's mercy and trust in the help of his grace.[322]

While some of the writers above were sometimes imprecise, possibly leaving the impression that they thought we had to work for our salvation, all of them would insist that salvation is by grace through faith, but that genuine faith involves a heart change that produces a life change. The point of this historical overview is to show that this teaching

---

320   Arthur W. Pink, *"Signs of the Time," Studies in the Scripture*, 16:373-375; quoted from John MacArthur. *The Gospel According to Jesus*. Rev. ed. (Grand Rapids : Zondervan)
321   A.W. Tozier, *I Call it Heresy!* (Harrisburg, Pa. : Christian Publications, 1974), 18-19; quoted from John MacArthur. *The Gospel According to Jesus*. Rev. ed. (Grand Rapids : Zondervan), 271.
322   The *Catechism of the Catholic Church*, New York : USCCB, #1431.

on genuine faith is not some new, strange doctrine, but is in
fact, core Christian doctrine, taught by prominent Christian
teachers, preachers and theologians—both Catholic and
Protestant—since the time of Jesus himself.[323]

We have seen that one of the main themes of all
four Gospels is about Jesus the Christ, the God-king, King
of all kings, coming to his people with his good news of the
kingdom. This story is brought to a climax in all four gospels
with Jesus being executed for claiming to be the King of that
kingdom, and then being vindicated by his resurrection from
the dead! The New Testament teaches that our King is a an
all-wise and compassionate King who loved us so much he
submitted to torture to save us! He now calls us to repent of
our sin and to turn him in loving devotion, following him in
obedience, which is our reasonable service.[324] This devotion
results in a desire to do those things which we know—from
the study of His Word—will please our King; and to avoid
those things which will not please our King.

We know from Scripture that attitudes and behaviors
pleasing to our King would include striving toward a lifestyle of
love, joy compassion, mercy, kindness, generosity, forgiveness,
prayer, worship, encouragement, humility, morality, honesty,
peace-making, evangelism, disciple-making, defending the
faith, and building others up in the faith.

Among those attitudes and behaviors which are not
pleasing to our King include idolatry, (i.e. putting anything
before God), murder (or abortion), hatred, immorality
(including pornography, sex outside of marriage and having
sex with people of the same sex), any kind of occult practices
(witchcraft, fortune telling, spells, séances, Ouija boards,

---

323   All of these quotations came from John MacArthur's book *The Gospel According to Jesus*. Rev. ed. (Grand Rapids : Zondervan), and are only a sample of the quotations he provides in that excellent book.
324   Cf. Romans 12:1-2.

etc.), self-centeredness, arrogant pride,[325] malicious gossip, drunkenness and substance abuse, stealing, dishonesty, cheating, lying, et al.

In short, we are to love our King more than we love to live. We are to love our neighbor as we love ourselves, avoid sin like the plague and sincerely repent when we fail—and unfortunately, we will fail. Those who call themselves Christians, however, and do not sincerely desire to live a life pleasing to God are deceiving themselves. Unless they repent they will find themselves among those to whom the King says, "Depart from me you evil doers, I never knew you."

As the prominent author/pastor Francis Chan (1967-　) says, "He wants all or nothing. The thought of a person calling himself a 'Christian' without being a devoted follower of Christ is absurd."

325　　　The sin if pride is often misunderstood. It is not necessarily sinful to take pride, for example, in the accomplishments of one's children, grandchildren, parents, brothers, sisters or friends. This is inferred from the fact that Paul took pride in his churches (1 Thessalonians 1:4; 2 Corinthians 9:2). It is not necessarily sinful to take pride in one's own accomplishments. One of the blessings of the future millennial kingdom is that people will be able to have a sense of pride in the work of their hands which others will no longer steal or destroy (Isaiah 65:21-23). According to the *Evangelical Dictionary of Theology*, sinful pride is an "Inordinate and unreasonable self-esteem, attended with insolence and rude treatment of others..." (874). I would add that sinful pride is an attitude of arrogantly taking all the credit for things and failing to acknowledge and give glory to God for his work in our lives and accomplishments.

Conclusion

When someone enlists in the military they take the following oath:

> I...do solemnly swear (or affirm) that I will support and defend the Constitution of the United States against all enemies, foreign and domestic; that I will bear true faith and allegiance to the same; and that I will obey the orders of the President of the United States and the orders of the officers appointed over me, according to regulations and the Uniform Code of Military Justice. So help me God.

The demands placed on some of us in the military were not all that strenuous. Sure, we had to endure basic training and sometimes there were long hours and "war games" but most of our enlistment—at least for those of us who were Air Force crew chiefs—was not all that different from a regular job. For other members of the military, life is significantly different. Many are called to leave family and friends, live in uncomfortable, if not downright deplorable circumstances, and face terrifying dangers. Some get shot. Some are permanently maimed. Some are tortured. Some lay down their lives.

As far back as high school, many years ago, I have been fascinated by the Special Forces—especially the Air Force pararescue jumpers or PJ's. PJ's are special forces-trained medics. According to the book, *None Braver*, the training for PJ's is so demanding that they have a higher dropout rate than the Green Beret or Navy Seals![326] PJ's regularly risk their lives, often going behind enemy lines, to rescue and provide medical

---

326   Hirsh, Michael. *None Braver*. Amazon Kindle version, New York : NAL Trade. 2004. Location 5682 (Chapter 12).

care to those who need it. In fact, their motto is, "That others may live." PJ's are trained to be ready for anything. They will go anywhere, face any danger, endure any hardship, and suffer any trauma "that others may live."[327]

In some ways, being a Christian can be likened to being in the military. Our ultimate commander in Chief is our King of kings and our Constitution is the Bible. Although salvation is completely by grace, our King expects our allegiance (faith). Just like those in the military, all Christians will face trials, stresses and hardships. Like everyone else in the world, there will be Christians who must endure painful illness, accidents, disability, divorce, unemployment, abuse and other trials. We may never know why these things happen but what we know is that God calls us to be faithful.

Just like in the military, some will be called upon to face more severe hardship than others. For example, as a teenager, Joni Erickson Tada had a tragic accident that left her paralyzed from the neck down. Life for her has undoubtedly been incredibly difficult. She may never know, this side of eternity, why God allowed this accident to happen. What she does know is that God calls her to be faithful. And she has been! In spite of her disability, she has had an amazingly productive

---

327   This does not mean, however, that Christians should always stay in situations of suffering or persecution if other options are available without being unfaithful to the Lord. For example, there were times when even Jesus hid himself or ran away to escape persecution (e.g. John 8:59; Luke 4:28-30). In Damascus, Paul was let down over the wall in a basket to escape persecution (2 Corinthians 11:32-33) and in Jerusalem the believes put Paul on a boat headed back to his home in Tarsus to escape death threats (Acts 9:26-30). Paul also used the Roman legal system to escape a beating (Acts 22:22-25) and even potential death (Acts 25:1-11). On one occasion Peter miraculously escaped prison and went into exile to escape the danger (Acts 12:1-19). On the other hand, there were times when Jesus and the apostles knowingly and willingly went head-long into enormous suffering and even death (John 12:12-28; Acts 21:10-13). Similarly today, there may be times, for example, when missionaries are exposed to such danger that they pack up and leave—and that may be perfectly acceptable to God. Other missionaries may choose to stay with the people they serve and risk everything—and that may also be an honorable decision. There may also be times when Christians choose to move or change jobs to avoid suffering. Or sometimes they may choose to stay as a witness and face the suffering head-on. Sometimes Christians may even have to leave an abusive spouse, for example, out of concern for safety of the children. Such decisions require the kind of wisdom that can only come from God (see James 1:2-5).

ministry. Helen Keller was both blind and deaf. She may never have known why God allowed this. What she did know is that God called her to be faithful. And faithful she was! Her life has touched millions. Other Christians were born into alcoholic, drug abusing, dysfunctional or violent families. They may have endured terrible abuse when they were young. This side of eternity they may never know why. All they need to know is that God's calls them to be faithful and is there for them.

Other Christians may be trapped in lonely, loveless marriages and stay solely because God calls them to be faithful. Some Christians are gay—the question of "why" is not necessarily all that important. The important thing is that God calls them to be faithful, so they live lives of celibacy out of love for their Lord. It is undoubtedly a very hard life.

Other Christians have given up everything in service to the King. They feed, clothe, provide medical care and share the gospel with people all over the world. Some of them have been beaten, imprisoned, tortured, and slaughtered for their faith. Like the PJ's, they were willing to face any danger and any situation "that others may live."

Just like Special Forces welcome this hardship and consider it an honor, so also Christians should consider the extra hardship an honor. Jesus said there would be great reward for those who endure insult and persecution for Him.[328] After the apostles had been beaten, they rejoiced that "they were counted worthy to suffer dishonor for the name."[329] Peter exhorted his readers not to "be surprised at the painful trial you are suffering, as though something strange were happening to you. But rejoice that you participate in the sufferings of Christ...."[330] Peter writes "For to this [suffering] you have been called, because Christ also suffered for you,

328 Matthew 5:11-12.
329 Acts 5:41.
330 1 Peter 4:12-13.

leaving you an example, so that you might follow in his steps."[331] James tells his readers to "Consider it pure joy... whenever you face trials of many kinds."[332] Contrary to the "health and wealth" heresy, following Jesus may not always result in personal prosperity in this world.

The kind of Christianity that treats God as a heavenly genie who exists to answer our prayers, a God who would never want us to be unhappy, is a modern idol. We may call him "God" or "Jesus" but this god is neither. He is no less a myth than Santa Claus and no less an idol than Baal. The fact is that we have a God who may call on us to endure enormous, almost unbearable, hardship and suffering—but who promises that the most horrible torture we could possibly endure will not even be worthy to compare to the incredible, unbelievable glory He has in store for us.[333] We can choose to believe him, or not. We can choose to be faithful or not.

According to the Bible, we have a King—our ultimate Commander-in-Chief—who desires our absolute allegiance and faithfulness. Although we are weak and will often fail—like Peter who declared his undying allegiance to Jesus, only to deny him shortly thereafter—our striving and goal should always be to please our King and to be faithful to him regardless of the situation in which we find ourselves. We should strive to live a life worthy of the great calling we have received,[334]—to be holy as he is holy[335]—not in order to be saved, but because by His grace through faith, we have been given the amazing privilege of serving the King of Kings and Lord of lords.

---

331   1 Peter 2:21.
332   James 1:2.
333   Romans 8:18.
334   Ephesians 4:1; Col 1:10; 1 Thessalonians 2:12.
335   1 Peter 1:15.

May the God of peace, who through the blood of the eternal covenant brought back from the dead our Lord Jesus, that great Shepherd of the sheep, equip you with everything good for doing his will, and may he work in us what is pleasing to him, though Jesus Christ, to whom be the glory forever and ever. Amen (Hebrews 13:20-21).

Postscript

If, having read this book, you realize that you are among those to whom Jesus will say, "Depart from me, I never knew you," I urge—as Peter once did—to "Repent and be baptized...in the name of Jesus Christ for the forgiveness of your sins."[336] Baptism is like the public renouncing of ultimate allegiances to other "gods" in your life (and even your own self-centeredness) and the public expression of ultimate loving devotion and allegiance to (i.e. faith in) your new Lord, the King of kings. Or, to put it in more biblical terms, baptism is the public expression of your "death" to sin and your "resurrection" to new life in Christ.[337] Baptism doesn't save anyone, but if someone refuses to take the first step of allegiance to the King, there is reason to doubt whether that one has genuine faith or allegiance to the King at all.

---

336   Acts 2:38; cf. Colossians 2:12; 1 Peter 3:21.
337   Romans 6:1-6; cf. Galatians 2:20.

Bibliography

Boston, Thomas. "A Brief Explication of the First Part of the Assembly's Shorter Catechism," in *The Complete Works of the Late Rev. Thomas Boston, Ettrick*, 12 vols. Wheaton, IL : Roberts, 1980 reprint.

Calvin, John. *Institutes of the Christian Religion* edited by John T. McNeill. Philadelphia : Westminster Press, 1960, III.2. 8.

The *Catechism of the Catholic Church*. 2nd ed. Washington, DC : USCCB Publishing, 1995.

Criag, William Lane Craig and Gerd Ludemann. *Jesus' Resurrection; Fact of Figment?* Edited by Paul Copan and Ronald K. Tacelli. Downers Grove, IL: IVP Press, 2000.

Crossan, John Dominic and N.T. Wright. *The Resurrection of Jesus; John Dominic Crossan and N.T. Wright in Dialogue*. Edited by Robert B. Stewart. Minneapolis : Fortress Press, 2006.

Dillenberger, John, ed., *Martin Luther*. New York : Doubleday, 1961.

Ehrman, Bart D. ed. *The Apostolic Fathers* (Loeb Classical Library). Cambridge, MA : Harvard University Press, 2003.

Evans, Craig and N.T. Wright. *Jesus the final days*. Louisville, KY : WJK Press, 2009.

Gill, John. *A Body of Divinity*. Grand Rapids : Sovereign Grace, 1971.

Griffith Thomas, W.H. *St. Paul's Epistle to the Romans*. Grand Rapids : Eerdmans, n.d.

Habermas, Gary R. *The Historical Jesus; Ancient Evidence for the Life of Christ*. College Press, 1996.

Habermas, Gary and Antony Flew. *Did Jesus Rise from the Dead; The Resurrection Debate*. Eugene, OR : Wipf and Stock, 2003.

Habermas, Gary and Michael Licona. *The Case for the Resurrection of Jesus*. Grand Rapids : Kregel, 2004.

Harris, Murray. *Jesus as God; the New Testament Use of Theos in Reference to Jesus*. Eugene, OR : Wipf & Stock Pub., 2008.

Hendriksen, William. *Romans (New Testament Commentary Series)*. Grand Rapids : Baker, 1981.

Hirsh, Michael. *None Braver*. Amazon Kindle version, New York : NAL Trade. 2004.

Hodges, Zane. *Absolutely Free; A Biblical Reply to Lordship Salvation*. Grand Rapids : Zondervan, 1989.

Holmes, Michael, ed. *The Apostolic Fathers*. 3rd ed. Grand Rapids : Baker, 2007.

Kostenberger, Andreas. *A Theology of John's Gospel and Letters*. Grand Rapids : Zondervan, 2009.

Licona, *Michael R. The Resurrection of Jesus; A New Historiographical Approach*. Downers Grove, IL : IVP, 2010.

MacArthur, John. *The Gospel according to Jesus: What is Authentic Faith*. Rev. ed. Grand Rapids: Zondervan, 2008.

Manschreck, Clyde L. ed. and trans., *Melancthon on Christian Doctrine*. Grand Rapids : Baker, 1965.

McDonald, Lee Martin. *The Story of Jesus in History and Faith*. Grand Rapids : Baker, 2013.

Matera, Frank, J. *God's Saving Grace; A Pauline Theology*. Grand Rapids : Eerdmans, 2012.

Richardson, Cyril C. ed. *Early Christian Fathers*. New York : Macmillan, 1970.

Roberts, Alexander and James Donaldson, eds. *Ante-Nicene Fathers*. 10 volumes. Peabody, MA : Hendrickson, 1885, 1995.

Robinson, James M. The Nag Hammadi Library. Rev. ed. San Francisco : HarperSanFrancisco, 1988.

Shaw, Mark. *Great Ideas from Church History*. Downers Grove, IL : IVP Press, 1997.

Spurgeon, Charles H. *The Soul Winner*. Passadena, Tex. : Pilgrim, 1978.

Stoesz, Samuel. *Sanctification; an Alliance distinctive*. Camp Hill, PA : Christian Publications, 1992.

Strobel, Lee. *The Case for the Resurrection*. Grand Rapids : Zondervan, 2010.

Tabor, James D. *Paul and Jesus; How the Apostle Transformed Christianity*. New York : Simon and Schuster, 2012.

Torrey, R.A. *How to work for Christ*. Old Tappan, NJ. : Revell, n.d Van Voorst, Robert. *Jesus Outside the New Testament*. Grand Rapids : Eerdmans, 2000.

Tozier, A.W. *I Call it Heresy!* Harrisburg, Pa. : Christian Publications, 1974.

Vanderkam, James C. *The Dead Sea Scrolls Today*. Grand Rapids : Eerdmans, 1994.Vincent, Thomas.

The Shorter Catechism of the Westminster Assembly Explained and Proved from Scripture. Edinburgh : Banner of Truth, 1980.

Whitefield, George. *Journals.* Edinburgh P: Banner of Truth, 1960.

Wright, N.T. *How God became King.* New York : HarperOne, 2012.

---. *The New Testament and the People of God.* Minneapolis : Fortress Press, 1992.

---. *The Resurrection of the Son of God.* Minneapolis : Fortress Press, 2003.

About the Author

Dennis Ingolfsland, M.A., M.A.L.S., D.Phil., is Director of Library Services and a full-tenured Professor of Bible at Crown College in Minnesota. He is also the pastor of Valley View Baptist Church in Shakopee. A veteran of the United States Air Force, he has a B.A. in Biblical Languages from Calvary Bible College, an M.A. in Library Science from the University of Missouri in Columbia, an M.A. in Theological Studies from Fuller Theological Seminary and a D.Phil. in Religion and Society from Oxford Graduate School in Tennessee.

In addition to his first book *The Least of the Apostles*, Dr. Ingolfsland has published three ebooks, *Clement of Rome, Salvation by faith or works?*; *Jesus, Muhammad and Fundamentalism*; and *The Third Quest for the Historical Jesus; a bibliographic guide.* His Blog, THE RECLINER COMMENTARIES is a commentary on news, current events, social issues and religion [www.ReclinerCommentaries.com].

Travels have taken him through almost every state in the lower 48, as well as to numerous countries including, Mexico, Canada, England, Germany, Israel, Egypt, Jordan, Turkey, Greece, and Iran. He is happily married to Sheila who has a degree in management and ethics from Crown College, and takes care of their granddaughter with Down Syndrome full time. They have three children and eight grandchildren.